THE CARIBBEAN

THE CAR

A WELCOME BOOK

TEXT AND PHOTOGRAPHS BY

BILL SMITH

IBBEAN

ESSENCE OF THE ISLANDS

Bulfinch Press · Little, Brown and Company · Boston Toronto London

ADDITIONAL PHOTOGRAPHY BY Amie Katz Smith
on pages 20, 36, 41 (top right), 42, 57
(top and bottom), 61, 62 (top), 68, 71, 76, 83,
90, 98, 127, 145, and 155 (right) and
the back flap.

Produced by
Welcome Enterprises, Inc.
164 East 95 Street
New York, NY 10128

DESIGNER: Nai Y. Chang
EDITOR: Timothy Gray

First edition

ISBN 0-8212-1745-3

Library of Congress Catalog Card Number: 89-
42901

Bulfinch Press is an imprint and trademark
of Little, Brown and Company (Inc.)

Published simultaneously in Canada by
Little, Brown & Company (Canada) limited

PRINTED IN SINGAPORE

SPONSORS

I am extremely grateful to the following corporations,
whose integrity and dedication to quality have helped me
make my dream of this book into a reality.

AMERICAN EXPRESS

DIVI HOTELS

KODAK

QUALITY COLOR LAB

A special thanks to American Airlines,
the Caribbean Tourism Organization, Marcella Martinez Associates,
the tourist bureaus of the islands featured in the book
and their public-relations firms,
and Lena Tabori, Nai Chang, and Tim Gray
at Welcome Enterprises.

BARBADOS

This book is dedicated to my wife and friend
AMIE KATZ
who helped with much of the work that went into it
and who shared my hopes, fears, and joys every step of the way.
A constant source of moral support,
she was also a thorough researcher and tireless production manager,
tending to thousands of details with consummate professionalism.
Without her effort, this book would have been far less than it is.
I also dedicate this to my grandmother

GOLDIE SELLY
whose love, strength, and unique character
have been an inspiration in my life.

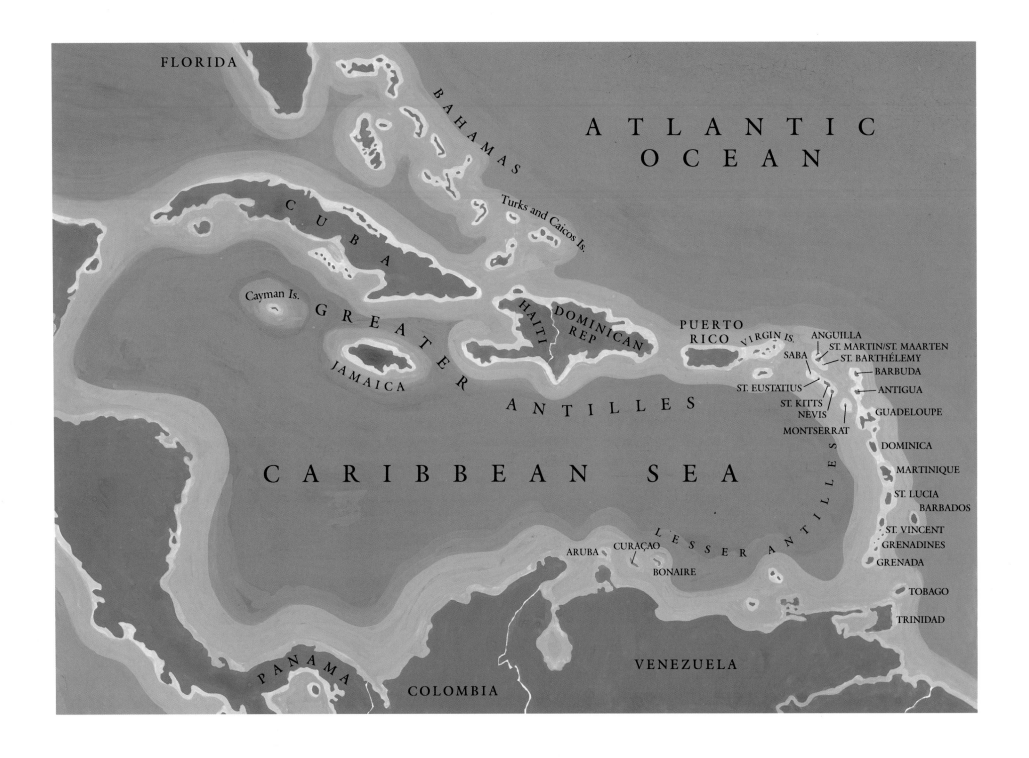

CONTENTS

BAHAMAS

ST. LUCIA

ESSENCE OF THE ISLANDS

This book provides a look at one of the most beautiful and serene parts of the world. I have found that people who are unfamiliar with the Caribbean assume it to be one big sea filled with islands that are basically all the same. Certain images usually come to mind: sun-drenched beaches, tranquil blue waters, gentle tropical breezes rustling through coconut palms fringing the shore. While it's true that visitors will find these things without ever leaving the confines of their seaside hotels, the islands have a great deal more to offer. They are steeped in history, filled with cultural riches, and rife with natural wonders that would add considerable dimension to anyone's idea of a perfect vacation. What's more, no two islands are the same. Some may share certain features with others, but the total picture is always different.

The purpose of this book is to provide a representative overview of the Caribbean region—information that will stimulate the reader's curiosity about the breadth of adventure available in the real Caribbean. This is not a guidebook in the traditional sense. Specific restaurants, hotels, and shops are rarely mentioned, and the reader will have to look elsewhere to find advice on making travel arrangements. Instead, various "essences" of a selected group of islands are presented in order to characterize the Caribbean as a whole. While a water sport such as windsurfing is featured in the section on Curaçao, and a craft such as batik-making is a focus on St. Kitts, this does not necessarily mean that these activities are unique to those islands. Some aspects—including the birds-of-prey show on St. Maarten, Jamaica's reggae festival, and the phosphorescent bay off one of Puerto Rico's satellite islands—cannot be found anywhere else in the Caribbean. But certain other features on one island lend something of the flavor that helps

ARUBA

diversity, especially in terms of topography, history, culture, ethnicity, and recreational opportunities. I wanted them collectively to present a thorough picture, so I included some islands that are popular among tourists and others that are less traveled. For research, I not only drew upon my own frequent visits to the islands but relied on valuable information provided by employees of tourist organizations, public relations firms, transportation facilities, and hotels that service the region. The islanders themselves were immensely helpful. I also consulted several individuals who have traveled extensively throughout the Caribbean. Once I felt that I knew enough about each island, I made my decisions.

As a group, the Caribbean islands extend from the tip of Florida in a 2,500-mile-long chain that arcs out into the Atlantic Ocean and hooks back along the northern coast of Venezuela. Many are part of a volcanic range that once linked North America with South America and is now primarily underwater. The entire Caribbean region lies south of the Tropic of Cancer, and trade winds that blow from the northeast serve as a welcome cooling factor. Most islands are blessed with year-round temperatures that range from 75 to 85 degrees Centigrade. In general, the summer months are rainy and the winter months are dry, but this varies according to each island's location.

Most historical accounts of the Caribbean begin in the late 1400s and early 1500s, when Christopher Columbus made four voyages to the area. Before his arrival, the islands were primarily occupied by a peace-loving tribe of Indians known as Arawaks, whose principle activities were farming, fishing, and making crafts. Unfortunately for them, a cannibal tribe from South America, the Caribs, seemed destined to follow them wherever they went. These hostile Indians were mostly exterminated by European colonists who settled in the years that followed.

Columbus made his four voyages on behalf of Spain. He was searching for a western sea route to India, and, when he arrived in the Caribbean, he thought he had found it. As a result, the region became known as the West Indies, and the Arawaks and Caribs were called

define another. For example, the quaint fishing village of Oistins on Barbados has its own personality, but its traditions and practices are reminiscent of other seaside towns. While views from the carefully designed trails that wind through Puerto Rico's El Yunque are uniquely scenic to that rain forest, the lush vegetation there is suggestive of teeming tropical growth elsewhere. And Carnival, while especially festive on Martinique, is celebrated just about everywhere.

Choosing the islands was no small task. The Caribbean Sea covers approximately one million square miles. Hundreds of islands are found here, most of which are small, uninhabited cays. There are 30-some major islands and island groups, and I selected ten to represent the Caribbean. My choices were based on each island's comparative

Indians. The Spanish explorers were primarily interested in precious metals and began finding them in South America. Other nations, particularly England, France, and the Netherlands, refused to accept Spain's sole claim on the New World and began both to establish colonies themselves and to plunder the treasure-filled Spanish galleons sailing back to Spain. In the 1600s, most Caribbean islands had been claimed by one of these four countries, all of whom spent the next two centuries trying to conquer and acquire each other's lands.

In the 1700s and 1800s, the islands became valuable sources of sugar, coffee, spices, fruit, and tobacco. African slaves were imported to work the plantations beginning in the late 1600s and continuing until the mid-1800s. Then slavery was abolished—first by the British in 1834, followed by the French in 1848 and the Dutch in 1863. In an attempt to keep the plantations thriving, indentured laborers were brought over from India, China, and other Asian lands. Today, the 30 million people who live throughout the Caribbean are the descendants of all these races—some the result of intermarriages, others with less mixed blood lines. Cultural ties to the various homelands remain strong, and the volume of languages spoken is vast—ranging from the familiar Dutch, English, French, and Spanish, to the numerous mixed dialects of Papiamento, Creole, and Patois.

The twentieth century ushered in a new trend: the shift toward decolonization. Some islands remain under European rule, but many have achieved total independence from their mother countries and others are moving in that direction. Newfound autonomy has forced the islands to fend for themselves in the marketplace. As a result, tourism as an industry—a fairly recent development—began to be promoted in the 1960s and has shown huge increases ever since. Even though sugar exports, which account for one fourth of the world's supply, contribute significantly, the Caribbean is still not as affluent as other areas in the western world. Even so, the poorer people who live here are proud, dignified, and kind. They are fully aware of the importance of tourism to their economies, and their respect for visitors seems genuine. In some of the outermost hamlets of the less developed

GUADELOUPE

islands, villagers may sometimes seem slightly unsociable, but this should not be mistaken for hostility. These people are simply not used to strangers and tend to channel their shyness by concentrating more intensely on whatever it is that they are doing. However, a simple smile is usually the only passport a traveler needs, for it will be returned instantly. Those who treat islanders with respect will receive the same courtesy in return.

"Caribbean time" is a common expression on the islands, and it refers to the relaxed style of living that islanders prefer. Because the sun is hot and the pace is slow, a pleasurable quality of life prevails. Caribbean people are not overly concerned with punctuality. This isn't to suggest that they are irresponsible; rather, it is to say that this part

HIBISCUS FLOWER

of the world has its own sense of time. People think in terms of morning, noon, and night, and, if someone shows up for an appointment half an hour late, it is not frowned upon. Everyone understands this, and visitors to the region who allow themselves a little extra time when traveling will find the concept of "Caribbean Time" very agreeable.

In the year it took to photograph this book, my wife Amie (who assisted me in every phase of the project) and I encountered hundreds of Caribbean residents within many cultures. They included fishermen and vendors, athletes and chefs, artists and government officials, and several are mentioned in the chapters that follow. All impressed us as people of substance, who expressed themselves eloquently, without

ST. JOHN

PRIDE OF BARBADOS FLOWER

artifice, and who seemed to know how to enjoy life to the fullest. Even though our time spent on the islands was constant hard work, filled with juggling the logistics of travel, researching and scouting locations, and lugging equipment from the predawn hours well into the night, we found the pervasive good will infectious. It was the most enjoyable year of our lives, made even more special by the fact that we got married while on Barbados. We made many friends, shared wonderful adventures, and absorbed a wealth of fascinating island culture. I'm sure that anyone who elects to travel to this enchanting region of the world will find that its "essences" are treasured experiences that are not soon forgotten.

13

ARUBA

The million square miles of Caribbean Sea are bordered on the west by Mexico's Yucatán peninsula, on the southwest by Central America, and on the south by Colombia and Venezuela. To the north, the larger Caribbean islands of Cuba, Jamaica, Hispaniola, and Puerto Rico form the island group known as the Greater Antilles. From the east coast of Puerto Rico down to South America are a group of smaller islands known as the Lesser Antilles. Because the upper half of this section sits directly in the path of the trade winds that blow from the northeast, they are called the Leeward Islands. The bottom half is known as the Windward Islands. Sometimes, the islands off the coast of South America are referred to as the Southern Antilles.

In addition to the islands that are discussed in the following chapters (as well as others off the Mexican and Venezuelan coasts), there are several major islands and island groups that deserve mention. In alphabetical order, they are:

ANGUILLA

Anguilla (Spanish for "eel," from the long and narrow shape of the island) is a British Associated State in the Leeward group of the Lesser Antilles. Anguilla seceded from St. Kitts and Nevis in 1967 and became self-governing in 1976. This flat island is made of limestone, has beautiful beaches, and receives scant rainfall. Sea salt mining, fishing (especially crayfish), and livestock raising are the mainstays. People visit for the peace and quiet that Anguilla offers.

ANTIGUA AND BARBUDA

Antigua and Barbuda, located in the Lesser Antilles, comprise another Associated State of Great Britain. Columbus discovered Antigua in 1493 and named it for the Church of Santa Maria la Antigua in Seville, Spain. The semi-arid island has frequent droughts on its hilly inland, while beautiful beaches line its greatly indented coast. It offers some of the best year-round weather, pottery and cotton-goods specialties, and several attractions for history buffs. Barbuda, thirty miles to the north, is an arid wilderness. A scuba diver's paradise, complete with some 50 to 60 shipwrecks, exists off this coral island's excellent beaches.

ARUBA

Aruba, discovered by Alonso de Ojeda in 1499, is an arid island that lies outside the Caribbean hurricane belt. The majority of the world's aloe was produced here in the first half of the twentieth century. Although still technically a part of the southern Netherlands Antilles, Aruba has begun a process of separation from Holland and will be granted complete independence in 1996.

BAHAMAS

The Bahamas are approximately 700 islands and 2,400 uninhabited cays that extend 750 miles to the southeast, starting 50 miles from the tip of Florida. While the Bahamas are technically surrounded by Atlantic Ocean, they are similar in climate and spirit to the Caribbean community and are generally regarded as a part of it. Together, the islands form an Independent State within the British Commonwealth. The word Bahamas comes from the Spanish "baja mar," meaning "shallow sea," and the islands themselves are predominantly flat limestone and coral formations containing many mangrove swamps, great beaches, beautiful coral and fish, and no rivers. A great many shellfish and crustaceans are exported to the United States, and over 100,000 square miles of good sailing waters surround these islands.

BONAIRE

Bonaire, discovered by Amerigo Vespucci in 1499, lies in the southern Netherlands Antilles. This is an arid island, with one good harbor that is a major export point. Sisal hemp and salt are produced, and goats and sheep are raised. Bonaire is most popular among scuba divers (there are over 50 scuba diving grounds) and bird watchers (for its abundant bird population).

BRITISH VIRGIN ISLANDS

The British Virgin Islands lie in the Leeward group of the Lesser Antilles, to the immediate northeast of the U. S. Virgin Islands. Discovered by Columbus in 1493, this group is made up of over 50 very green islands, only 16 of which are inhabited. Tourists usually go to one of five principle islands: Tortola, Beef Island, Virgin Gorda, Anegada, and Jost van Dyke. Some of these islands used to be the haunts of pirates. Today, they are a self-governing Dependent Territory of Great Britain.

CAYMAN ISLANDS

The Cayman Islands, discovered by Columbus on his last voyage in 1503, are a British Crown Colony made up of three islands: Grand Cayman, Little Cayman (mostly a mangrove swamp), and Cayman Brac (from the Gaelic meaning "bluff"). They were originally know as the Tortugas for the great number of turtles found here. Except for one turtle farm on Grand Cayman, the reptile is now practically extinct in this region. Reputed to be some of the safest islands in the Caribbean, the Caymans' economy relies on tourism but receives a boost from ship building and exports of coconut and lumber.

CUBA

Cuba, discovered by Columbus on his first voyage, is, at 44,218 square miles, the largest island in the Caribbean. It also happens to be one of the few primarily Spanish islands in the region. Several dances were born here, including the conga, the rumba, the tango, and the mamba. The capital of Havana was once a popular American gambling center, but the revolution in 1959 changed that. Today, Cuba is the only socialist republic in the Caribbean, and travel restrictions are usually in effect. Some of the Western Hemisphere's most challenging deep-sea waters can be found here.

DOMINICA

Dominica, an independent country in the Windward group of the Lesser Antilles, was discovered by Columbus in 1493. This is a hilly island with magnificent mountain scenery and over 350 rivers and streams. Many fumaroles (volcanic crevices issuing hot vapors) can be viewed here, and most of the island is covered with dense rain forest. Formerly the world's largest producer of lime concentrates, bananas are now the chief export. Dominica is the site of the world's only Carib Indian reservation.

DOMINICAN REPUBLIC

The Dominican Republic, discovered by Columbus on his first voyage in 1492, occupies the western two thirds of the Greater Antilles island known as Hispaniola. (Haiti occupies the eastern third.) This is the most mountainous of the West Indies, and frequent earthquakes subject the terrain to upward thrusts. Economically, the island is predominantly agricultural, with sugar cane the major crop. The Dominican Republic has an uncommonly turbulent history, but the government is more stable today. The merengue dance was born here. The capital city of Santo Domingo is the oldest city in the Americas.

GRENADA

Grenada, along with the southern half of the Grenadines archipelago, is an Independent State within the British Commonwealth located in the Windward Islands of the Lesser Antilles. Discovered by Columbus in 1498, Grenada is famous as "The Spice Island" because of the nutmeg, mace, and other spices grown there. The island was invaded by U. S. forces in 1983 as a result of tensions surrounding the construction of an international airport backed by Soviet-supported Cuba. Today, the island has veered away from its flirtation with Marxism.

GUADELOUPE

Guadeloupe is a French overseas département in the Windward Islands of the Lesser Antilles. Some political groups there today are trying to gain complete independence from France for the island. The capital city of Basse-Terre, founded in 1640, is one of the oldest French colonial towns in the Caribbean and serves as the government seat for the entire French Antilles islands. Guadeloupe is actually two islands separated by a narrow channel, with a hilly, volcanic western section and a flat limestone eastern half. Sugar cane and bananas are the economic staples, and over half of the residents are under the age of 20, indicating the population explosion that Guadeloupe has seen in recent years. Cockfight viewing is a popular recreational activity here and can be found in almost every village.

HAITI

Haiti is an independent republic occupying the eastern third of Hispaniola (with the Dominican Republic to the west). In the nineteenth century, the lumber industry destroyed many of Haiti's natural forests, and today very little of the land is agriculturally productive. Coffee is the biggest export, and some of the best crafts in the Caribbean can be found here. Considered to be the poorest country in the Western Hemisphere, mostly because of the population density, Haiti also has one of the lowest crime rates. Approximately 85 percent of the population practices voodoo.

MONTSERRAT

Montserrat is a tiny British Crown Colony in the Windward Islands of the Lesser Antilles. Formed by three volcanoes, the island is hilly and provides some terrific landscapes for climbers and hikers. Columbus discovered it in 1493, naming it after a similarly shaped mountain mass northwest of Barcelona. Soufrière, Montserrat's highest peak, is a dormant volcano and major tourist attraction.

SABA

Saba is a Windward Island in the Lesser Antilles that belongs to the Netherlands (although many of its inhabitants are of Scottish descent). This circular island is actually the exposed cone of an extinct volcano, so there are no beaches and no harbors to speak of. Saba is perhaps the most topographically unusual island in the Caribbean. Life begins halfway up the island, and the chief settlement, called The Bottom, is at the top of a plateau. Vegetables and fish are the chief economic staples.

ST. BARTHÉLEMY

St. Barthélemy is a French island in the Windward group of the Lesser Antilles. Columbus discovered it in 1493 and named it after his brother. Commonly known as St. Barts, this is a small and quiet island with a pastoral atmosphere. The villages, full of trim little houses, are particularly quaint, and the residents, unlike most Caribbean islands, are primarily white.

ST. EUSTATIUS

Discovered by Columbus in 1493, this Netherlands Antilles island is in the Leeward group of the Lesser Antilles. Known more commonly as Statia, it is mountainous and one of the Caribbean's more unspoiled islands. A volcanic cone known as The Quill dominates the southern region. Life here is simple and

HELICONIA FLOWER

relaxed. St. Eustatius was supposedly the first foreign port to salute the American flag in 1776.

ST. LUCIA

St. Lucia is an Independent State within the British Commonwealth, located in the Windward Islands of the Lesser Antilles. Britain and France fought bitterly for this island, because both wanted to take advantage of the heavy shipping traffic that passed through. St. Lucia has many inlets, one of the most beautiful natural yacht harbors at Marigot Bay, and twin volcanic mountains known as the Pitons. This island served as a location for many James Bond films, has the only drive-in volcano in the world, and is unusual

in that it's not known for certain who discovered it (although it may have been Columbus on his last voyage in 1502).

ST. VINCENT AND GRENADINES

St. Vincent and the northern islands of the Grenadines comprise an Independent State in the British Commonwealth. St. Vincent is west of Barbados in the Windward group of the Lesser Antilles and is composed of volcanic rock. Because of its diverse natural beauty, it has been nicknamed both "The Emerald Isle" and "The Pearl of the Antilles." The Grenadines lie to the south of St. Vincent and are defined by eight large and over 120 smaller islands (10 are inhabited). They form one of the world's finest sailing areas.

TRINIDAD AND TOBAGO

Trinidad and Tobago were joined politically in 1888 and became an Independent Nation in the British Commonwealth in 1962. Columbus discovered them on his third voyage. Located off the northeast coast of Venezuela, these are the most southern and among the most exotic of all Caribbean islands. Large reserves of oil make petroleum and petroleum products the principle export and give these two islands one of the strongest economies in the Caribbean. Trinidad, composed of 45 races—mostly African—is where the calypso, the limbo, and steel bands originated.

TURKS AND CAICOS ISLANDS

Geographically, these islands are a southeastern continuation of the Bahama Islands. Discovered by Ponce de León in the early 1500s, they form a British Crown Colony today. The Turks and Caicos Islands are a small archipelago of over 40 tiny islands. The few that are inhabited are secluded. Economically, the islands are supported mainly through crustacean and shellfish exports. Miles of reefs make this region one of the best spots in the Caribbean for scuba diving.

BARBADOS

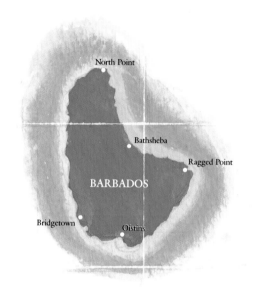

North Point

Bathsheba

Ragged Point

BARBADOS

Bridgetown

Oistins

Sleepy Sunday, perhaps better dubbed "national recovery day" for Saturday-night revelers, is a time when kids can bikeride through Speightstown (north of Bridgetown on the Gold Coast) without the usual distractions of cars and crowds.

BARBADOS

Every island in the Caribbean has at least one distinctive quality that lingers in each visitor's memory. In Barbados, it is the people. Called Bajans or Barbadians, they impart a sense of humor, intelligence, pride, and natural curiosity that is disarming. Not only are they hospitable, known to go so far as to share their homes and food, but they are also an industrious group, who never lose sight of their ability to enjoy themselves. With a population of over a quarter million, the collective warmth of spirit is infectious.

Barbados is the easternmost island in the Caribbean, lying about 100 miles east of St. Vincent. Completely surrounded by the Atlantic Ocean, it is one of the few islands not discovered by Columbus. Presumably, Portuguese explorers arrived in the early 1500s, naming their discovery "Los Barbados," "the bearded ones," after the exposed, hairlike roots of the fig trees along the shores. The Portuguese did not settle here, but the British did a century later in 1627, when Holetown became the first colony. British rule lasted 339 years, making Barbados the only Caribbean island able to claim unbroken ownership. On November 30, 1966, it became independent, even though some inhabitants today like to call it "Little England."

The island's 160 square miles have a coral limestone base, causing Barbados to be relatively flat. The highest point, at Mt. Hillaby in the north-central part of the island, is only 1,115 feet. The rest of the

Three beach vendors carry their wares to a new location.

inland is rolling hills, dry valleys, sugar cane fields, and tropical vegetation. Tranquil waters and beautiful beaches on the south and west coasts have attracted the most development for tourism, while the jagged bluffs and pounding surf of the windy east coast show off nature's more dramatic side. Sugar and tourism form the commercial base, but exports of molasses, syrup, and rum also contribute significantly to the economy.

Like most islands in the Caribbean, Barbados is home to hundreds of hotels that provide tourists with a wide selection, from superluxurious resorts to simple inns. Restaurants offer such indigenous fare as fresh tropical fruits, spicy island soups, and many seafood specialties, including the favorite flying fish, whose delicate taste is served up in several ways. Exotic cocktails, such as the rum-charged Barbados Bombshell, are also popular. Some of the best paved roads in the Caribbean and one of the world's purest water supplies are just two more components that help characterize the highly civilized standard of living here.

PAGE 17:
Bridgetown, capital of Barbados and rife with shopping opportunities, is a mixture of modern offices and colonial architecture. Bridgetown's basin, called The Careenage, pictured here, used to be where schooners were "careened" so that their hulls could be cleaned, painted, and repaired. The main commercial thoroughfare of Broad Street ends here. Also visible (to the right of center) are Trafalgar Square and the former House of Assembly.

EDUCATION

The level of education in Barbados is the highest in the Caribbean. With a literacy rate of 97 percent, Bajans take understandable pride in their scholarship, no matter what their ambition or eventual role in community life. Schooling is mandatory until the age of 16, and anyone who passes the necessary exams is allowed to go to college at no charge.

Formal education aside, Bajans like to stay well informed and up-to-date. The genuine thirst for knowledge that is inherited at an early age seems to last a lifetime. Their interests extend to world affairs—a fact reflected by the presence of both foreign and local reading material on the newspaper stands. Radio and television broadcasts provided by the British Broadcasting Corporation are eagerly received.

Schools are as excellent as they are diverse. Queens College, founded in 1818, is one of the island's leading secondary schools, while the modern Cave Hill University serves as the training center for police throughout the Caribbean. Visitors will find all Bajans stimulating conversationalists—quick-witted, politely to-the-point, and civilized in their unlimited zeal for information.

LEFT:

Codrington College, in St. John Parish near Consett Bay on the east coast, is named for Christopher Codrington III, whose bachelorhood ended a family line that lived on Barbados since 1642. When he died in 1710, he bequeathed 10,000 pounds for the formation of a "Society for the Propagation of the Gospel." After a lengthy legal battle with family members in England, the society came into existence some 38 years later. It is one of the earliest institutions of higher education in the Western Hemisphere. Today, with its palm-lined avenue leading to the original coral stone buildings, it is a stately theological seminary.

OPPOSITE:

A vast, manmade lily pond greets the visitor at the entrance to Codrington College.

HARRISON'S CAVE

Harrison's Cave, near the valley town of Welchman's Hall Gully in central Barbados, is actually a series of underground caves. Rediscovered in 1970 by Ole Sorenson, a Danish speleologist who surveyed and mapped the area for the Barbados National Trust, the caves began to be developed for tourism in 1974. Tunnels were dug, the caves were painstakingly surveyed, and drainage and lighting problems were resolved. The most arduous task was diverting the two streams that ran down the center of the passageway.

Today, the caves are fully excavated. Tours, which have been available to the public since 1981, are preceded by informative slide shows about the history of the caves and the geological formations that will be seen. Anecdotes about how the caverns were discovered add to the excitement when the trip gets underway.

Once a tour begins, as many as thirty passengers board a tram that is pulled down a mile-long track into the caves by means of an electric car. Going from one cavern to the next, the tram sometimes stops while a guide points out something of particular interest. Except for the headlights of the tram and spotlights placed to showcase certain formations, the cave is pitch black. Visitors are simultaneously engulfed by darkness and awestruck by the areas they are intended to see. Stalagmites and stalactites, forming at a rate of one cubic inch every 123 years, loom from above and below everywhere. Each new sight assumes its own personality: one group of formations might seem like an enchanted fairy-tale land, while another

might take on the appearance of several frogs squatting at the edge of a wading pool. Every new location teases the imagination.

There is a dampness in the atmosphere, but it doesn't emit the dank smell that might be expected. The air is clean and fresh, even as the tram rounds each corner and delves deeper into the caves. At one point, it travels through a huge cavern— approximately 250 feet high—with a ceiling that glitters like a crystal chandelier. At another juncture is the still beauty of a silent subterranean pool, lying just a short distance from a thundering waterfall. A visitor could go through the caves many times and spot something different on each outing. It is a wonderful adventure to experience a cavernous world that has taken millions of years to form and is still changing, even as each new sightseer passes through.

As the first light of dawn hits the water, a local fisherman wades out to his boat to begin another day's work. His catch might include shark, dolphin, barracuda, snapper, and, of course, the ever-popular flying fish.

OISTINS

Oistins is a southern coastal village, where, in 1652, the natives pledged their loyalty to Oliver Cromwell by signing the charter of Barbados at the Ye Mermaid Inn. Situated on a bay of the same name, Oistins is and always has been the major fishing community of Barbados. For generations, it was also the social center of the southern coast. Although there has been change over the last two decades—with shopping centers beginning to make their presence felt—the sea remains the center of the town's life. The two-day Oistins Fish Festival every April pays tribute to the skills of the fishermen and women with such activities as fish boning, boat and crab races, and eating from food stalls. The rest of the year, typical sights include the making and mending of fishing nets, the painting of boats, and the preparing of fish.

Aside from its economic importance to Oistins, the fishing industry provides natives and visitors with the Bajan delicacy, the flying fish. This delicious, sweet-tasting food has become a national symbol. Not only does it appear in beachside sandwiches and several gourmet dishes, but the fish's likeness seems to adorn everything, from clothing and flags, to tableware and craftworks.

A former shipping port, Oistins still functions today as the primary location for building and repairing fishing boats.

Whether played with international-class standards or in a more impromptu, less ceremonious manner, a cricket match can always be found on weekends. This game was part of a divisional "knockout" tournament held at Foundation Hall in Oistins.

CRICKET

Two sports have caught fire in the hearts of the Bajans: cricket and soccer. June through January is the recognized cricket season, and January through June gives soccer its official turn, but informal matches in both sports seem to flourish year round.

Cricket is by far the national obsession. Played on a large field with two wickets 22 yards apart, the object of the game is to score runs by batting the ball far enough so that one player is able to exchange wickets with the batsman defending the opposing wicket before the ball is recovered. Bajans are so devoted to this sport that those unable to watch television during a game can be seen with transistor radios glued to their ears, their concentration hanging on every play.

International cricket matches are held at Kensington Oval, where capacity crowds of 15,000 can always be expected. Barbados has produced more world-class cricketers per square inch than any other country in the world. One Bajan player, Sir Garfield Sobers, set such a high standard of play that he was knighted by Queen Elizabeth II and now serves as a role model against which other players measure themselves.

Cricket was introduced to the island by the British military over 200 years ago. In 1877, the first club, the Wanderers, was formed. The game was then and is now an embodiment of some of the most noble values of Britain: good sportsmanship, gentility, and a relaxed formality. The phrase "to play cricket," meaning "to play fair," was coined from this game.

The Animal Flower Caves in North Point are named for the sea anemones that grow underwater and in pools on the rock walls. Nicknamed "sea eggs," these anemones are popular Bajan delicacies. For a small fee, a guide will lead the curious down a winding stairway to the sea caves. Those who don't mind getting their feet wet can wade through small pools to the spot where the anemones grow.

27

Manuel, after his leap, collects snails at North Point.

AUTHOR'S EXCURSION: NORTH POINT

In order to get to North Point, the northernmost part of Barbados, we had to venture off the main road and follow the signs. When we arrived, we were lucky enough to participate in an adventure that is not included on any of the regular tours but is typical of the Bajan hospitality anyone would encounter.

Only one business exists in North Point: a thatched, A-frame snack bar. We walked in and immediately noticed thousands of business cards adorning every inch of available space on the walls and ceiling. The establishment is owned and run by twin brothers, Winston and Manuel Ward. We spoke with Manuel, a congenial and colorful Bajan soul whose natural intelligence has been enhanced by a good formal education. He explained that the business cards were collected from visitors in order to indulge a fantasy that he and his brother might someday be mentioned in the Guinness Book of World Records.

A friend of Manuel agreed to guide us down the sheer cliffs of North Point to the sea pools at the base. The ocean here has battered the 60,000-year-old coral base of the island into sea caves, and there is much to explore. As we climbed down, Manuel closed the snack bar and congregated with a small group of his friends at the top of one cliff. We reached the bottom and looked up to see him jump off into one of the pools—a place we later learned often contains sharks.

Emerging from the pool, Manuel invited us to join him for an impromptu meal. He scavenged for snails, then built a fire in order to cook them. While the snails cooked, we drank beer, talked, and took in the beauty of the secluded surroundings. The snails could only be eaten by cracking their hard shells with a rock. Primitive perhaps, but they were as sweet and tasty as any that can be found in a gourmet restaurant.

CLOTHING DESIGNERS

There are three clothing designers on Barbados whose stylish creations are as suitable for the Caribbean as they are for urban cities everywhere: Derek Went, Carol Cadogan, and Simon. All three create clothes that have a flowing, free feeling, and two of them are represented by boutiques in Bridgetown in addition to having their own places. But that is where the similarity ends.

Derek Went's designs reflect his personality: earthy, easygoing, and fluid. His showroom, located in his home, overlooks the ocean near the eastern coastal town of Bathsheba. Horses roam his front yard, while his glassless windows look out over palm trees. A pet monkey resides near the workroom, where Derek dyes and batiks his multilayered garments by hand. One example of his work, patterned after an African butterfly and colored with iridescent blues and greens, is designed so that when the arms are lifted the fabric spreads like a butterfly's wings.

Carol Cadogan's works of "wearable art" are sold at her boutique, Petticoat Lane, on the wharf in Bridgetown. She is best known for her white, one-of-a-kind outfits made of 100 percent cotton and adorned with appliqué collages of silk, satin, leather, and lace.

Simon, whose work is not pictured here, uses soft, flowing cottons and rayons. His boutique, full of sophisticated jungle prints and tie-dyed styles, is located on the Gold Coast north of Bridgetown as well as on the neighboring island of Mastique.

Derek Went's designs (opposite) are internationally shown, with prices ranging from as low as $50 to
a high of $1,200 and over. He receives interested
shoppers by appointment. Carol Cadogan also has
a loyal international clientele. The outfit pictured
(left) is a more fiery version of the style that has
made her name well known.

ST. KITTS-NEVIS

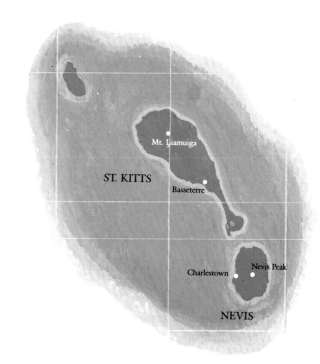

Mt. Liamuiga

ST. KITTS

Basseterre

Charlestown   Nevis Peak

NEVIS

Frigate Bay on the southeast peninsula is a white-sand beach, considered to be one of the best on St. Kitts. It boasts both a windy side that faces the Atlantic Ocean and a calmer side on the Caribbean Sea. This area of the island has been set aside for resort development.

St. Kitts-Nevis is an independent nation located in the eastern Caribbean. These two islands, with Nevis lying to the south of St. Kitts, are separated by a two-mile-wide channel known as The Narrows. Charlestown is the capital of Nevis, but Basseterre, capital of St. Kitts, serves as the government seat of both islands.

Columbus discovered these islands on his second voyage in 1493, naming Nevis "Las Nieves" (Spanish for "the snows") after the snow-white cloud atop its single peak. He reputedly named St. Kitts, officially called St. Christopher, in honor of the patron saint of travelers, although there is some speculation that he named the island after himself.

The native Carib Indians retained control of the islands for over a century after Columbus. Then, in 1623, the English founded their first colony on St. Kitts, which shortly thereafter was nicknamed "The Mother Colony of the British West Indies" when it served as a base from which settlers went out to colonize Antigua, Barbuda, Tortuga, and Montserrat. The French arrived in 1625, and a year later the island was divided between Britain, who controlled the central mountainous part of the island, and France, who claimed the northern and southern lowlands. These two nations led an acrimonious coexistence with periodic bloodshed until 1783, when the Treaty of Versailles recognized St. Kitts as a British possession. Nevis was settled by the British in 1628. St. Kitts-Nevis became completely independent in 1983.

St. Kitts is dominated by a central mountain mass that begins to rise at the sea's edge and peaks at 3,792 feet at Mount Liamuiga. ("Liamuiga," meaning "fertile island," was the Caribs' original name for St. Kitts, while "Oualie," meaning "land of beautiful water," was

PAGE 33:

On the northeast coast of St. Kitts, just off the main road, is an area known as Black Rocks. These oddly shaped formations were created when Mt. Liamuiga's lava hurled and burned its way down into the Atlantic Ocean in prehistoric times.

The work day on St. Kitts ends at 4:00 p.m., and, by 4:30, soccer has begun. To the spectators and participants of this most popular sport on the island, only the game matters, not the playing conditions.

their name for Nevis.) The entire island of Nevis is one fairly symmetrical volcanic circle, with Nevis Peak climbing to 3,232 feet. Today, St. Kitts has 65 square miles and Nevis covers 36, but it is thought that they were once connected eons ago.

There are approximately 40,000 people living on St. Kitts and 12,000 on Nevis—mostly descendants of Africans. Kittitians and Nevisians alike are genuinely friendly—so much so that a tourist who has parked his car to take photographs might be asked by other motorists if he needs assistance. Most people live in coastal towns and villages around each island's perimeter, since inland the steep slopes cannot be cultivated beyond a certain height.

Agriculture is the chief industry, with sugar cane the foremost crop on St. Kitts and sea-island cotton and coconuts the primary

staples of Nevis. Tourism, the second major industry, has grown considerably in recent years, especially on St. Kitts. The vegetation is so lush here that it overwhelms the senses, and Kittitians are wisely protective of their unspoiled paradise. In an attempt to preserve the environment, development has been sanely planned and limited primarily to the southeastern peninsula, where the island's finest beaches can be found. Nevis offers its tourists more teeming greenery, long white-sand beaches, offshore coral reefs, and a solid dose of peace and quiet. The outside world just fades away, and time really seems to stand still.

Nevis is a 45-minute ferry ride from St. Kitts, with ferries usually docking twice daily in Charlestown. This is a charming town with colonial architecture, quaint shops, and narrow side streets. Within walking distance are the Alexander Hamilton Museum, the beautiful Pinney's Beach, and the Bath Hotel, whose hot mineral springs was once the spa of choice for eighteenth-century European aristocracy.

A short walk through a coconut grove leads to the palm-lined beach at Dieppe Bay. This town is on the northern coast of St. Kitts, where the Atlantic Ocean meets the Caribbean Sea. Like the other beaches on the upper portion of the island, the sand at Dieppe Bay is gray—a testimony to the volcanic flows of many years ago.

OPPOSITE:
Dieppe Bay, once a landing area for slaves, was occupied by the French for most of the seventeenth and eighteenth centuries. It was named for the French Normandy town of Dieppe on the English Channel. Today, Dieppe Bay is a fishing village that offers pleasant swimming and snorkeling opportunities. The beach is also a popular picnic spot for visitors who like to rent a car and go sightseeing along the well paved road that circles St. Kitts and passes through most of its coastal towns. Two interesting establishments in the vicinity are Gibson's Pasture estate, which was once a sugar mill and fort, and the elegant Golden Lemon hotel, run by Arthur Leaman, a former editor of House and Garden, *who has individually decorated each room in grand style.*

The road to Romney Manor and Caribelle Batik travels up a steep slope, through a tropical rain forest, and onto the well tended grounds of the former plantation. Nature's star attraction here is the huge Saman tree—sometimes called a rain tree—which is said to be over 350 years old.

BATIK

Caribelle Batik is a business that is based in Romney Manor, a restored seventeenth-century great house located a short distance from the town of Old Road on St. Kitts's southern coast. The high-quality batik that comes out of its workroom is the result of an intricate and time-consuming process. The technique was first developed over 2,500 years ago in Indonesia. The batik procedure begins by sketching a design onto a white cotton fabric. The sea-island cotton that makes the material is grown locally and is reputed to be the finest in the world. Next, a mixture of hot beeswax and paraffin is applied with a tjanting tool—an instrument that resembles a wide-pointed pen. The wax serves as a dye repellant during the coloring stage. While Caribelle Batik exports its goods all over the Caribbean, it also sells them in showrooms adjoining the working area.

LEFT:
Visitors are permitted to enter the workroom at Caribelle Batik and watch the batik-making process. Color is applied either by painting the fabric, as shown here, or by dipping it into the dye.

BOTTOM:
Large sheets of batik-dyed cloth are hung outdoors to dry. Nowadays, top-quality dyes hold their colors and don't bleed in the wash. The cloth will be sold both raw and in finished goods such as scarves, dresses, shirts, and wall hangings.

The parade is a colorful assemblage of uniformed groups that includes soldiers, police, musicians, constables, scouts, and Brinks security guards.

September 19th is a special date for the people of St. Kitts-Nevis. On that day in 1983, the islands gained complete independence as a country within the British Commonwealth. Prior to that time and since 1967, St. Kitts-Nevis was an Associated State of Great Britain. This meant that, while it independently governed its internal affairs, foreign matters were handled by the mother country. (Anguilla, several miles to the north, helped form this State until 1981, when it became a British territory.) Kennedy A. Simmonds, then Premier of St. Kitts-Nevis, led the dependency to nationhood and, in the elections of 1984, became its first Prime Minister. The government today is based on the British system, with elections held every five years.

We took part in the Independence Day festivities of September 19, 1988. We were told that this particular celebration was especially energetic because it hallmarked the fifth anniversary of self-government. Nevisians and Kittitians began to congregate in Basseterre early in the morning. People filled the stands or found trees, grassy knolls, and walls on which to perch. Officials made their entrances and took their seats. The parade and review of troops began at 8:30 a.m., and, for nearly two hours, participants marched, bands played military tunes nonstop, and the assembled troops were reviewed by the highest officials of St. Kitts-Nevis.

After the parade, the crowds dissolved into the streets to celebrate. Picnics, planned parties, and impromptu get-togethers flourished throughout the afternoon, with live bands and disc jockeys controlling the air waves.

Troop leaders are on hand to orchestrate military movements. An extended arm with an upraised sword is a gesture that holds the troops at attention.

LEFT:
Soldiers march toward the review stand, where they will salute government officials and move into formation.

OPPOSITE:
Two prerequisites for any large celebration: sneakers and speakers.

BRIMSTONE HILL

On the western coast of St. Kitts, atop a hill that rises approximately 800 feet, looms the magnificent fortress at Brimstone Hill. Known as Fort George, this structure consists of five bastions made from lava rock and is spread out over thirty acres. Molasses, lye, and horse hair were the mortar that helped assemble it, and its walls are several feet thick.

Nicknamed "The Gibraltar of the West Indies" for the mammoth rock beneath it, the fortress was built by the British as protection against the French. Slaves began construction in the late 1600s and took nearly one hundred years to complete their labors. Overpowered by the French in 1782, the British were able to reclaim it the following year.

A steep, zig-zagging road, created by the Royal Engineers centuries ago, snakes its way up to Fort George. Sometimes called The Citadel, the fort now houses a museum that offers segregated displays of British, French, Arawak, and Carib history. Outside, on a clear day, the islands of Saba, St. Eustatius, St. Barts, St. Martin, Montserrat, and Nevis can be seen in the distance. To the east lie the rain forests that blanket the mountains.

On October 23, 1985, Queen Elizabeth paid a Royal Visit to St. Kitts and officially designated Brimstone Hill as a national park and monument. It is the main tourist attraction on the island and one of the most impressive sights in the entire Caribbean. In terms of size and architecture, the fort rivals many in Europe and leaves anyone who sees it with a sense of respect for those who engineered it. A testament both to man's greatness and the folly of war, visitors today find it a perfect place to sit, picnic, and be lulled by the beauty of the world around them.

NEVIS ACCOMMODATIONS

Tourist accommodations on Nevis are much different from the modern hotel and motel chains found on other islands. Most places here are restored great houses and sugar mills that are more reminiscent of country inns than anything else.

Nevisian guest-house owners pride themselves on the impeccable service they offer visitors. In an informal, elegant, and slow-paced style, they enjoy trying to keep everyone happy. Guests operating under the honor system are usually free to help themselves to drinks when the bartender is not around. They are entrusted to sign a ledger that will let the proprietor know to charge it to their bill. Or they might be allowed to freely borrow from bookshelves. It's not unusual for a host or hostess to dine with the guests, promoting an easy camaraderie. Most guest-house owners will selflessly recommend another inn's dining room as a good place to eat. After-dinner activities on this quiet island might include a game of backgammon, watching television, or a talk with other guests. It is a civilized and relaxing experience, no matter where a visitor chooses to stay.

Pinney's Beach is located about a mile north of Charlestown on Nevis's western coast. With three miles of sand, clear waters, and a sleepy lagoon, it is the best beach on Nevis. Palm trees grow so tall here and on the rest of Nevis that signs warn visitors to avoid parking their cars under potentially falling coconuts.

The Hermitage Plantation, in the Fig Tree Village area of Nevis, is typical of the country-inn style of accommodations. It is a partially restored plantation with several acres of gardens. Originally, the property was the residence of the Colonial Agricultural Officer, who used the grounds as a place to test and develop new varieties of fruit trees, from lime, avocado, mango, and cashew, to breadfruit, bay cocoa, sugar apple, guava, and pau-pau.

Hermitage Plantation has a main building as well as several guest houses, each with two floors, a kitchen, a bedroom, two baths, and a balcony. The furnishings here are colonial antiques, and the rooms are usually filled with fresh flowers that have been picked on the grounds.

JAMAICA

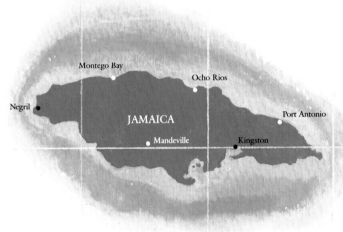

Montego Bay

Ocho Rios

Negril

JAMAICA

Port Antonio

Mandeville

Kingston

"Out of many, one people" is Jamaica's motto—an apt reference to a population of two and a half million that was created by intermarriage among many races. Approximately 95 percent of the mix has an African or Afro-European origin, with the remainder primarily British, German, Portuguese, Middle Eastern, Indian, Chinese, and South American. The people have a straightforward manner that is tempered by a gentle and witty sense of humor that most visitors find disarming.

After Columbus discovered Jamaica in 1494, the Spanish settled and retained power until the British took over in 1655. Two decades later, British pirates based themselves on the island in order to attack Spanish ships and ports. One famous buccaneer, Henry Morgan, befriended Jamaica's governor and eventually became the island's lieutenant-governor. British rule ended on August 6, 1962, when Jamaica became an independent nation, maintaining only loose ties to the Commonwealth.

Lying 90 miles south of Cuba in the Greater Antilles, Jamaica could well be the most beautiful island in the Caribbean. At 4,411 square miles, it is the third largest. The Arawak Indians who originally lived here called their land "Xaymaca," meaning "place of waters and woods," but this only hints at the topographical diversity. Jamaica has it all: dark green mountains and valleys, magnificent waterfalls, idyllic coves and bays, and over 200 miles of white beaches. Hundreds of species of birds, ferns, orchids, and other flora and fauna abound— many of them unique to Jamaica. Crops grow quickly and plentifully here in tropical forests and on rolling pastureland. Sugar cane, bananas, pimentos, and coffee are just some of the agricultural riches that help make Jamaica one of the few Caribbean islands completely self-sufficient in terms of food production.

PAGE 49:
At dawn, the fishermen have already left to begin their day's work. One wife stands repairing a net at the edge of the bay between Montego Bay and Ocho Rios.

Rose Hall Great House is located nine miles east of Montego Bay. Built in 1770 atop a ridge, this former sugar plantation has been stunningly restored. Although the three-story building is one of the most impressive on Jamaica, it is probably the legend of Annie Palmer that draws most people to it. Annie was the young wife of John Palmer, Rose Hall's builder and original occupant. She murdered him and her two successive husbands— each in a different bedroom and by a different method. She also reputedly took slaves as lovers at various times, killing them when she grew tired of their company. Although none of her homicides took place in her own bedroom (pictured), Annie herself was slain in bed here during the slave revolts of 1833. Believed to have been schooled in the arts of voodoo by a Haitian priestess, Annie's ghost, known as the White Witch, is said to haunt Rose Hall today.

OPPOSITE:
Harmony Hall, east of Ocho Rios, is a nineteenth-century Victorian-style great house that has been beautifully restored. Opened in 1981, it contains a restaurant and pub on the ground floor, an art gallery that showcases leading Jamaican talent, and a shop that sells some of the best crafts on the island.

Of Jamaica's six major cities and towns, the only one inland is Mandeville, a 2,000-foot-high mountain village in the west-central region. It has quiet, English-country charm, copious gardens and grounds (including Jamaica's only village green), and temperatures cool enough to make it the citrus center of the island. Kingston, on the eastern side of the southern coast, is Jamaica's bustling capital city of commerce, politics, and culture. The other four major spots are resort towns spread across the northern coast, where the best beaches can be found: Negril, at the western tip is a carefree, hedonistic community that boasts a seven-mile stretch of beach and mandates that no building be higher than the tallest palm tree; Montego Bay, in the northeast, is Jamaica's busiest tourist draw, with a wide range of resorts, restaurants, and attractions, three championship golf courses, and an international airport; Ocho Rios, on the central north coast, offers elegant hotels and exquisite natural settings; and Port Antonio, in the northeast, is the most secluded resort area, providing some of the best deep-sea fishing off its ragged, volcanic coast.

Throughout Jamaica, there is a special energy not felt on other islands. Things seem constantly in motion, whether it's a gentle breeze rustling the trees, rivers coursing down the mountains, or people in transit. Mostly, it's an intangible "aliveness." The island has a pulse, a vibrancy, and its rhythm touches the souls of both its people and its visitors.

Marshall's Pen, in the mountain town of Mandeville, was an eighteenth-century coffee plantation. Today, the great house's antique furnishings are available for public viewing. Outside, a cattle farm is maintained on the willow-covered grounds, where horses graze and several endemic species of birds freely dwell.

Jamaica's finest example of classic architecture is the stately Devon House. Located in Kingston, the mansion was built in 1881 by George Stiebel, one of the Caribbean's first black millionaires. Bought by the government and restored by the Jamaican National Trust in the 1960s, today it is the home of the National Gallery of Art (an African art and history museum) and is filled with exquisite, late-nineteenth-century furnishings. The extensive grounds, situated on the waterfront, hold former stables that have been converted into several high-quality crafts shops.

Kingston, Jamaica's capital city since 1872, sprawls from the base of the Blue Mountains to the sea, covering an area of 40 square miles. The city was founded in 1692 by the survivors of a devastating earthquake in Port Royal, the small breakwater town across Kingston's harbor. Today, with over 700,000 residents, Kingston is the largest English-speaking city in the Caribbean. Its natural harbor is the seventh-largest in the world. Although Kingston is crowded and commercial, it is Jamaica's center for business, government, education, and culture. Tourists usually head for the smaller resort towns on the north coast, but those who decide to give Kingston a whirl find an exuberance and enthusiasm that fills the air. Reggae music, originating in storefronts, bars, and restaurants, usually echoes through the streets in counterpoint to the swiftly moving traffic and bustling sidewalks.

An integral part of Jamaican life is entertaining family and friends during the weekend. As a result, market crowds are thickest every Thursday through Saturday, when everyone stocks up on provisions. Outdoor markets exist throughout Jamaica, with suppliers traveling long distances to sell their produce and wares. Traditionally, men handle the cultivation of crops and the manufacture of such items as baskets and clay bowls, while women are responsible for selling to the customers. As vendors, they are known as higglers, which comes from price haggling that is expected with every sale.

Goats stake a claim on an abandoned home near Ocho Rios.

57

A father and son, who take care of horses at the Chukka Grove Equestrian Centre near Ocho Rios, await the call for fresh horses at Drax Hall, the center's polo field.

Polo is a game that resembles hocky on horseback, played with mallets and a ball instead of sticks and a puck. Dating back to the time of the colonists, the game is a British tradition that has found its place among Jamaica's elite. Even Prince Charles comes here to play. Pictured is one moment in a tournament between the best women players in the world, hosted by the Kingston Polo Club.

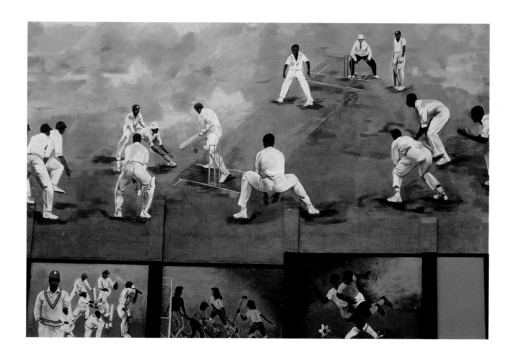

A mural on one wall of National Stadium, in Briggs Park, Kingston, reflects the cricket, soccer, and baseball that are played inside. Murals all over Jamaica, as well as throughout the Caribbean, tend to depict real-life events and activities of the neighborhoods in which they are painted.

In the rocky west end of Negril are many ledges and overhangs. Rick's Café is also here—a casual outdoor restaurant where, every night, just about everyone in the area makes a pilgrimage to partake in the nightly ritual of drinking cocktails, eating dinner, and watching the sun set. For many, jumping off the café's cliffs into crystal clear waters is also on the agenda.

One of the guides at Great River runs across a group of docked rafts to see about securing new passengers for another trip. When that trip is over and his passengers have disembarked, his work will only be half done: he must then walk his raft back up the river to the starting point.

RIVER RAFTING

Jamaica has over 120 natural rivers and streams. Three that course their way down the mountains to the shores—the Rio Grande in Port Antonio, the Martha Brae in Falmouth, and the Great River in Montego Bay—offer unique rafting opportunities for people of all ages. River rafting as a recreation is said to have been originated by American movie star Errol Flynn, who used to own a home in Port Antonio. The 30-foot-long bamboo rafts were originally used to transport bananas from plantations to freighters before overland shipping took over. The Rio Grande is Jamaica's largest river and offers the most dramatic ride. The three-hour trip covers about 8 miles of rapids and only slows down during the last leg of the journey. The Martha Brae and Great River rides are shorter and calmer. Rafts accommodate two passengers, who sit at the back end; a guide, who stands at the stem, navigates with a long pole. All trips flow through tantalizing rain forests, past such common sights as women washing clothes and men fishing along the shores. The guides are informative, skilled, and very attuned to the comfort, interests, and needs of their passengers.

DUNN'S RIVER FALLS

Two miles west of Ocho Rios is Dunn's River Falls, a 600-foot-high mountain stream that rushes over a natural stone "stairway" and flows into the Caribbean Sea. This is Jamaica's most spectacular waterfall, and visitors come to climb it. The first stop is the changing room at beach level. Then, under the leadership of experienced guides, small groups begin their ascent by walking right into the water and up the falls. When the footing gets tricky, most hold hands, but the more adventurous like to break away and discover their own routes up. The half-hour climb through the series of cascades and natural pools attracts thousands every year. Obliging guides are frequently asked to take photographs and are often seen with several tourists' cameras slung around their necks.

AUTHOR'S EXCURSION: REGGAE SUNSPLASH FESTIVAL

Every year in the middle of August, Jamaica hosts the world's largest reggae music festival. Called Sunsplash, it runs for six consecutive nights and, with a different line-up each evening, showcases some of Jamaica's finest musicians. Crowds include spectators from all over the world and number as many as 75,000 people per night. For four of these mellow, rhythm-filled evenings, we joined them.

Reggae music, characterized by a unique use of rhythmic accent, was born in Jamaica. Reggae lyrics often reflect religious views, denounce social evils, and put forth political demands. Although the music tends to celebrate the dignity of the black race, it transcends racial barriers and has found popularity in the international music scene. Direct reggae influences can be found today in the music of superstar performers like The Police, Paul McCartney, Paul Simon, and The Rolling Stones.

The person credited with creating reggae—and certainly the one most responsible for its popularity—is Bob Marley, who has had a profound effect on the Jamaican people. Because he represented reggae to the world as the people's music, he is a national hero today. In 1981, thousands, including most top government officials, came to pay their respects as he lay in state in Kingston—dead from cancer at the age of 36. At that year's Sunsplash, Stevie Wonder sang a song of tribute to Marley's memory.

When reggae was first introduced a few decades ago, the Jamaican government limited its radio play

to the dawn hours for fear that the music's political messages might reach the larger population. Ironically, reggae's raw, pulsating music is heard everywhere today and has come to symbolize the unique Jamaican energy and way of life. Kingston has become known as a "Third World Nashville"—mainly thanks to Tuff Gong International (the recording studio in Kingston that Marley built) and other facilities like it.

Reggae Sunsplash takes place at the Bob Marley Performing Center in Montego Bay. The music began each night at about 9 PM, and we usually arrived shortly thereafter. The atmosphere was informal and easy, with spectators staked out on various spots throughout the huge grassy grounds in front of the stage. Lining the roads were souvenir stands and record vendors as well as food shacks serving up such popular Jamaican fare as barbecued "jerk pork" and grilled spicy fish and chicken. As the music played, with one group immediately following another, the crowd got mellower. Some danced, while others sat and watched or lay back on blankets and soaked up the music's special cadences. Every program—a different one each night—lasted until noon the next day, when we would leave, pleasantly exhausted and completely sold on this distinct sound of Jamaica.

OPPOSITE:

On a hill overlooking Ocho Rios and the coast is a natural retreat known as Shaw Park Gardens. A former plantation site, its 34 acres now contain footpaths that lead visitors alongside waterfalls, streams, and ponds and through manicured grounds containing flowering gardens and majestic trees.

High on a hill in the north-coast town of Port Maria is the former retreat of Sir Noel Coward, who lived on Jamaica for the last 25 years of his life. The Jamaican government has kept everything exactly as it was on the day in 1973 when the famous writer and actor died. Named Firefly after the glowing insects that populate the property, the four and a half acres here include Sir Noel's modest tomb (pictured), a small house, and an open patio that commands an impressive view of the sea. Sir Noel's devotion to the creative process was so singular that he maintained another house at the bottom of the hill where his meals could be prepared without disturbing his concentration. Some of his famous guests here included Laurence Olivier, Katharine Hepburn, Winston Churchill, and Queen Elizabeth.

Crafts are sold everywhere on Jamaica, whether in shops, market stalls, or improvised stands. Independent vendors set up concessions along well traveled roads as well as on beaches and near tourist attractions. Pictured in this Montego Bay outlet are two of the more prevalent commodities: casual resort wear and straw goods.

OPPOSITE:
At Montego Bay, a fisherman collects sea urchins that he will later use as bait. For many Jamaicans, hunting the waters is a trade that has been inherited from previous generations.

OVERLEAF:
As the sun sets off of Montego Bay, a few lingering fishing boats point their stems home. Their catch will most likely include marlin, tuna, kingfish, and wahoo. Fishing is especially good several miles off the north coast of Jamaica in the Cayman Trench, a long gamefish passageway that connects the Atlantic Ocean with the Caribbean Sea.

PUERTO RICO

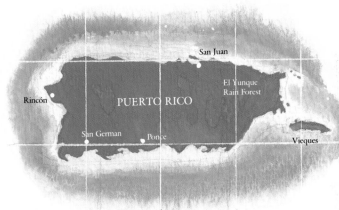

San Juan

Rincón

El Yunque
Rain Forest

PUERTO RICO

San German   Ponce

Vieques

Old San Juan's wall, built in the 1630s, used to surround the entire city but is now missing an inland section. The structure is actually two parallel 40-foot-high walls made of sandstone block, with sand filling the space between them. A 12-foot thickness at the top widens to 20 feet at the base. Pictured in the center of the wall is the San Juan Gate, first opened in 1639. Made of heavy wood, it is one of six gates that used to provide the only means of entering the city. Every sundown, the gates were closed. Above the wall and to the right of center is La Fortaleza, originally a fortress built to protect the Spanish settlers from the Carib Indians. For over 400 years, this building has been the residence and office of Puerto Rico's governor. It is said to be the Western Hemisphere's oldest executive mansion still in use.

Puerto Rico was originally named San Juan in honor of the patron saint of Juan Ponce de León, the Spanish explorer who accompanied Columbus when he sighted the island in 1493. Shortly after that time, Ponce de León became the island's governor and established its first colony on an eastern harbor section of the north coast. He called this settlement Puerto Rico (Spanish for "rich port") but later decided to switch its name with San Juan's, making Puerto Rico the island and San Juan the town.

In 1897, Puerto Rico achieved autonomy under Spanish rule, but Spain surrendered it to the United States a year later at the end of the Spanish-American War. The U. S. Congress granted Puerto Rico American citizenship in 1917, and, in 1952, the island became a Commonwealth of the United States. Today, Puerto Ricans choose to remain self-governing, even though they have a standing option to become America's fifty-first state.

Almost a third of the island's 3.5 million residents live in the San Juan metropolitan area. This capital city is the economic and cultural center of Puerto Rico. With an international airport and a ranking as the number-one cruise-ship port in the Caribbean (over 700 ships dock annually), it also receives most of the island's tourists. Modern highrise hotels and office buildings in fashionable settings contrast with the preserved colonial architecture of Old San Juan, a centuries-old section of the city that is protected as a national monument.

Topographically, three fourths of Puerto Rico's 3,435 square miles are mountainous. A dramatic and lush south-central range spans the island in an east-west direction, and lowlands and valleys run across the fertile northern and arid southern coasts. Sugar cane, coffee, and livestock farming used to form the economic base of the island; while these agricultural products are still important, the manufacturing of such products as chemicals and electronic equipment now contributes more. Stone, sand, and gravel mining, tuna fishing, and the production of rum (Puerto Rico's national drink) are also big. The island is home of Bacardi, the most popular rum in the world.

Castillo San Felipe del Morro, commonly known as El Morro, is a triangular fortress named after King Philip III. The word "morro" is Spanish for "promontory," and it refers to the fort's position 140 feet above sea level, right at the northwest tip of Old San Juan. The Spanish began constructing the fortress in 1540. Half a century later, additional work was done to protect the fort from attack by land. Improvements did not really stop until the end of the eighteenth century. El Morro was attacked many times—mostly unsuccessfully. Today, it is under the administration of the U. S. National Park Service and is Old San Juan's most popular tourist attraction.

Puerto Ricans are fond of using the expression "en la isla," meaning "out on the island." It refers to tourist exploration on Puerto Rico outside San Juan and other major cities. The government encourages "en-la-isla" expeditions by maintaining well paved roads throughout Puerto Rico and through its state-owned, privately managed parador system. A parador is an inexpensive and clean country inn located outside a city—usually near an historic site or natural attraction.

Ethnically, Puerto Rico is a blend of Spanish, African, and Taino Indian (a now extinct Arawak tribe). Spanish is the official language. Although most people outside San Juan do not speak English, they are friendly and make every effort to communicate with non-Spanish-speaking visitors. Most of the residents are Roman Catholic—a fact reflected by the presence of traditional church plazas in the majority of towns.

In addition to shops and historic sites, Old San Juan contains several residences, many of which have belonged to their tenants' families for generations. This man stands on his balcony on a Sunday morning, watching the strollers below appreciate the old-world city that he calls home.

OLD SAN JUAN

Old San Juan is a small, picturesque town that has been restored by the Institute of Puerto Rican Culture. Built in 1509, it is the second oldest city in the Americas (after Santo Domingo in the Dominican Republic). The town is located on San Juan Island, a narrow islet at the westernmost part of San Juan, and is connected with the newer part of the city by three bridges. The buildings in Old San Juan illustrate typically colorful Spanish architecture from the sixteenth and seventeenth centuries. This historic zone is steeped in Hispanic culture, with many museums, churches, statues, and other landmarks concentrated in an area that covers less than half a square mile. Narrow, slightly hilly colonial streets—once dirt roads—are now paved with blue cobblestones that served as ballast in nineteenth-century ships from England. Some of these streets are closed to vehicular traffic. For shoppers, there is a large volume of high-quality boutiques carrying such items as artwork, crafts, clothing, and jewelry.

Colorful mosaics form a unique store façade in Old San Juan.

This shot from the top of the Caribe Hilton Hotel shows an area known as the Condado, a district in San Juan that was once an exclusive residential section. Now it is a popular and fashionable tourist area with highrise hotels, casinos, shops, and restaurants. The Condado extends onto a peninsula, the tip of which is connected by a bridge to Old San Juan.

78

By law, all casinos in Puerto Rico are contained within large hotels. Pictured is the elegant Sands Casino, the biggest on the island, located in the Isla Verde section of San Juan, a district that continues a chain of luxury hotels located in the Condado to the west.

The El Yunque Rain Forest, located in Puerto Rico's northeast sector, is a lush, mountainous area that covers 28,000 acres. Officially known as the Caribbean National Forest, it is commonly called El Yunque after a peak here that reaches over 3,400 feet. The name comes from a benevolent Indian spirit named Yuquiyú.

El Yunque is the only tropical forest in the U. S. National Forest System. On the average, five brief showers a day fall here, accumulating to over 100 billion gallons per year. Located about an hour from San Juan, the forest is Puerto Rico's second favorite tourist attraction. For the islanders, its natural coolness makes it the perfect place to go to escape the summer heat. The natural growth is unchecked, and the flourishing vegetation is home to some exotic rare-bird wildlife, including the nearly extinct Puerto Rican Parrot. The preserve is also a refuge for millions of coquis, the inch-long tree frogs that are Puerto Rico's unofficial mascot.

Thirty miles of footpaths wind their way past hundreds of varieties of trees, ferns, and flowers. Several trails offer special sights. One example is the rugged 12-mile-long El Toro Trail that leads hikers up to the 3,538-foot peak of El Toro (the highest in El Yunque) and back again. The National Park Service provides such extras as visitor guides and camping permits for those interested.

OPPOSITE:
This is a view of Puerto Rico's arid southern region, taken just off a four-lane highway that originates in San Juan, cuts through the mountains, and moves on to the city of Ponce. Once the highway descends from the lush flora of the mountains, the air becomes dry and the topography undergoes a radical change.

This view of La Mina Falls is taken from Big Tree Trail, one of dozens of scenic paths that go through El Yunque.

PONCE

Ponce, nicknamed "The Pearl of the South," sits in a west-central location on the southern coast. This is Puerto Rico's principle shipping port and second-largest city. Founded in 1692, it took its name from Ponce de León, Puerto Rico's first governor. It is a beautiful city, combining its original Spanish colonial architecture with more modern buildings of recent years. The Ponce Museum of Art is world-famous—not only for the impressive design of its art galleries but also for its hundreds of paintings and sculptures, many of them by internationally known artists representing most American and European schools of the past 500 years. The Parque de Bombas is Ponce's eccentric firehouse, painted black and red (the city's colors) and containing bright yellow firetrucks. Just outside of Ponce is the oldest cemetery yet found in the Caribbean. Located at the Tibes Indian Ceremonial Center, the burial grounds were excavated in 1975, uncovering human skeletons that date back to 300 AD. The placement of stones around the Tibes dance grounds was made before Columbus's arrival. These stones line up perfectly with the sun during equinoxes and solstices, raising speculation as to whether the grounds once served as an astronomical observatory. Neighboring Coffin Island offers excellent snorkeling and scuba diving opportunities. These attractions are all less than two hours' drive from San Juan, making Ponce a popular tourist destination.

Ponce has many plazas and parks. Pictured are some of the pruned India laurel, fig trees, fountains, statues, and benches that completely surround the Cathedral of Our Lady of Guadalupe. These grounds are so diligently maintained that the streets and sidewalks are swept and washed down every morning.

The Cathedral of Our Lady of Guadalupe was built in 1670 and is the focal point of Ponce's Plaza Las Delicias, the main town square.

Miguel Caraballo and his son, also Miguel, are two of a small number of Puerto Rican artists who create the masks worn in Ponce's Bejantes Carnival every February. The masks have origins in Africa, where they are donned to scare away evil spirits.

The masks are constructed by shaping plaster of paris over cardboard forms. Assembly is done in layers and painting requires several coats, prompting the artists to leave the masks in the sun to dry between each stage. This makes the process time-consuming, and larger masks sometimes take as long as a month to complete.

The Caraballos have extended their artistry beyond Puerto Rico. In 1985, they participated in a special exhibit at The Smithsonian Institute in Washington, D. C. On another occasion, they met the King of Spain and treated him to a private viewing of their work.

This mask, made by an unknown artist in Ponce, sports about 200 horns. According to Miguel Caraballo, Sr., who constructed a similar mask that now hangs in his home, a work this intricate takes about six months to create.

SAN GERMÁN

San Germán is a charming little Spanish town in the southwest section of Puerto Rico, named for Germaine de Foix, the second wife of King Ferdinand of Spain. Built in 1512, it was destroyed by the French in 1528 and reconstructed in 1570 on a location slightly inland from its original shoreline position. In the 1600s, San Germán and San Juan were the only two towns on Puerto Rico. San Juan eventually underwent radical development, but San Germán today is still untouched by modern times.

The Rio Camuy Caves are located on a 268-acre park in northwest Puerto Rico. The underground Camuy River carved into the limestone terrain to form the caves over a million years ago. Visitors accompany guides on an electric trolley that descends 1,200 feet into a ravine and delivers them at the cave's entrance. The guides lead an average of 1,500 sightseers per day along the manmade, mile-long trail. The cavern pictured is one of the more impressive sights, with a 200-foot-high ceiling and a width of half a mile.

San Germán's Chapel Porta Coeli ("Gate of Heaven"), built in 1606, is one of the oldest chapels in the Western Hemisphere. The brick steps and heavy doors pictured are just as they were nearly 500 years ago. Inside is a museum containing a magnificent collection of religious art, including paintings and ancient santos (wood carvings of holy figures).

SURFING

The best surfing on the island can be found at Rincón's half dozen reef-lined beaches on Puerto Rico's westernmost point. This is where the Caribbean Sea meets the Atlantic Ocean and waves are at their most powerful. Only skilled surfers come here, where waves often reach heights of 25 feet. Rincón hosts Puerto Rico's annual Professional Surfing Contest and is an occasional site for the World Surfing Championship.

OVERLEAF:
This Navy-owned beach is located on the north shore of Vieques. Civilians are allowed access only when training maneuvers are not in progress.

AUTHOR'S EXCURSION: VIEQUES

We boarded a ferry at the east-coast fishing village of Fajardo. Our destination: Puerto Rico's quiet island of Vieques, a two-hour trip away. At various times, this 20-mile-long strip has been an Arawak Indian home, a thriving sugar-mill community, and a haven for pirates. Today, a good two thirds of the island belong to the United States Navy, who acquired it during World War II. Much of the beach land on Vieques is either on or accessible by naval-base property. Most are quite beautiful—we particularly enjoyed the white sands of Red Beach and Blue Beach—but they were not our main reason for coming.

We arranged to be met that night by a man who would take us to Vieques' most unusual natural phenomenon—a phosphorescent bay on the island's north coast. After the sun had set, he picked us up at our hotel. A small motorboat was attached to the back of his truck, and, when we arrived at Mosquito Bay, he unloaded it onto the water. With four other sightseers onboard, we ventured into the night sea. Before long, we found what we were looking for: millions of microscopic flagellates that produce a chemical light whenever the water is disturbed. (Another, less bright phosphorescent bay is located just off Puerto Rico's southwest town of Parguera.)

We first noticed the luminosity in the boat's wake behind us. The guide stopped the motor and stomped on the floor, startling hundreds of fish, whose sudden departure produced a white-flash effect. Nearby, the ghostly forms of some swimmers shimmered as they glided by. I scooped some water into a small bucket and tossed it into the air, then watched as it splashed down with a sparkle. We were fortunate enough to spend our hour on the bay under a moonless sky, which allowed the glow to be more pronounced. It was an eerily beautiful magic act of nature, accompanied by only one regrettable fact: the light level produced by the flagellates never gets bright enough to make the phenomenon photographable.

ST. JOHN ST. CROIX

THE UNITED STATES VIRGIN ISLANDS

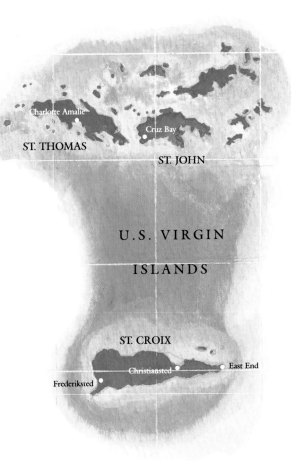

The license plates read "American Paradise," perfectly describing the three major U. S. Virgin Islands: St. Croix, St. John, and St. Thomas. Each one is beautiful and completely American—both in culture and in life style. St. Thomas, with its bustling shoppers and hopping nightlife, is the liveliest. Its waterfront town of Charlotte Amalie is the government seat for the entire group of over 50 islands, most of which are small, uninhabited cays. St. Croix and St. John, although slower-paced and less crowded, still claim tourism as the chief industry. More than a million visitors flock annually to these three islands, lured by white beaches, gem-colored waters, and duty-free shops.

Columbus discovered the U. S. Virgin Islands on his second voyage in 1493, naming them (along with the over 50 British Virgin Islands to the northeast) for the legendary 11,000 virgin martyrs who followed St. Ursula. The Virgin Islands lie several miles east of Puerto Rico. At various times, several countries—including Holland, France, England, Spain, Denmark, and Malta—have laid claim to one or more of these islands. In 1917, the United States bought them from Denmark for $25 million, when the sugar industry started to crumble and the U. S. wanted a Caribbean base from which to protect the Panama Canal. Residents today are U. S. citizens, although they cannot vote in federal elections.

OPPOSITE:

Fort Christiansvaern, in Christiansted on St. Croix, is the best preserved of five remaining Danish forts in the Virgin Islands. Built in the mid-1700s, it was garrisoned until 1878, when it became a courthouse and police headquarters. Its ocher-colored bricks served as ballast for ships that sailed from Denmark. Today, visitors can tour its battlements, kitchens, and dungeons as well as view Christiansted from the fort's walkways.

RIGHT:

The Annaberg Ruins is a partially restored sugar mill that provides the best glimpse of Danish plantation life in the 1800s. Self-guided tours take visitors along a looping trail and past such structures as a circular horse mill for crushing cane, bread ovens, a rum still, slave quarters, and a boiling bench that made brown sugar.

The St. George Village Botanical Garden is St. Croix's 17-acre master-ful combination of human landscaping and natural growth. Located near Frederiksted, this spectacle of tropical flora is situated among the ruins of the work houses and laborer homes of a nineteenth-century Dutch sugar cane village. Originally an Arawak Indian settlement, it was also once a cattle ranch before it achieved its current station in 1972. With an arcade of palm trees at the entrance, a stone dam, and a mean-dering stream adding to its magical beauty, it is also the site of occasional Sunday concerts and outdoor weddings.

The parrot flower is one of over a thousand varieties of flowers, trees, and vines found throughout the St. George Village Botanical Garden grounds.

Originally named Santa Cruz (Spanish for "Holy Cross") by Columbus, St. Croix, lying approximately 40 miles to the south of St. Thomas and St. John, is the largest and most southern of the U.S. Virgin Islands. With a population of about 60,000 and a land mass of 84 square miles, St. Croix offers the topographical diversity of a lush rain forest on the western side and arid, cactus-spotted terrain in the east. (The town of East End is the easternmost point in the United States.) Gentle, rolling hills and valleys cover most of the inland.

Differences can also be seen in the island's two main towns. Christiansted, on the north-central coast, is a picturesque town with the red roofs and pastel-colored buildings that are typical of seventeeth-century Danish architecture. The former capital of the Danish West Indies, Christiansted is full of intriguing boutiques, crafts shops, and outdoor cafés that help make it the tourist center of the island. In contrast, Frederiksted, on the west coast, is a sleepy port that only comes alive when a cruise ship is docked. Named in honor of Denmark's King Frederik V, this town's Danish buildings were ravaged by fire in the labor revolt of 1878. An ornate Victorian style of architecture, popular at the time, arose atop the stone arches that survived the blazes.

St. Croix's well paved roads and scenic vistas make self-guided car-rental tours popular among visitors. North Shore Road, South Shore Road, and East End Road wind around mountains, along coastlines, and over cliffs, while Centerline Road travels through the hills of former sugar cane plantations, now spotted with distilleries. Mahogany Road runs through a rain forest and alongside a mahogany woodworking mill, where a large variety of mahogany products are made and sold. Most routes lead eventually to St. Croix's pristine beaches, with names like Grapetree Bay, Cane Bay, and Sandy Point. All beaches are open to the public, and many offer excellent snorkeling and diving opportunities.

Although royal poinciana, commonly known as flamboyant trees, are found all over the Caribbean, they seem to be especially prevalent on St. Croix. A native of Madagascar, their brilliant orange-red blossoms bloom in summer, mixing with the bougainvillea, hibiscus, poinsettia, and frangipani to infuse the landscape with a radiant beauty.

several times to get a closer look at some of the fish. It took over half an hour to swim the route, but when we emerged again in the world of sound, it seemed as though we had only caught a quick glimpse into a wonderful aquatic jewelry box.

LEFT:
One of several boats that leave daily from Christiansted heads toward Buck Island.

OPPOSITE:
The Carambola Golf Course, near St. Croix's Davis Bay, was designed by Robert Trent Jones. Jones is the doyen of golf architecture and has designed over 500 courses worldwide, including several others in the Caribbean. Carambola, as difficult to play as it is beautiful, is one of the top courses in the world.

Located only six miles off the northeastern coast of St. Croix is Buck Island, American's only underwater national monument. Glass bottom boats and catamarans from St. Croix take visitors over calm waters for some peaceful picnicking on the uninhabited parkland and a snorkeling adventure through dazzling elkhorn coral.

We rented our snorkel gear through an organization known as Mile Mark Charters. After donning it, we started off on Buck Island's underwater nature trail. There are two major routes to follow: the Turtle Bay Trail and the East End Trail—both offering firsthand looks at the many-colored, multishaped forms of coral and the hundreds of varieties of tropical fish. Markers on the sea floor were informative and interesting, but it was the undersea silence that really made us take notice. The stillness seemed somehow to make everything more brilliant, more three-dimensional. I dove underwater

St. John, the smallest of the major U. S. Virgin Islands, is two miles east of St. Thomas and has a population of about 3,000. The British Virgin Islands lie to the north and east, and many can be seen from St. John's east coast. Today, St. John's land is an unspoiled hideaway of mountains and valleys, but this wasn't always so.

After St. John was colonized by Denmark in 1717, the Danes cleared the entire island for sugar cane plantations. Over a hundred flourished until the liberation of slaves ended the industry in 1848. Since then, St. John's natural tropical vegetation has reclaimed the island, and the ruins of former estates can sometimes be glimpsed underneath the growth.

In 1956, Laurance Rockfeller established the U. S. Virgin Islands National Park Service, which has kept preserved over two thirds of St. John's 20 square miles. Tourism, although the major industry, is concentrated in a few small areas.

St. John's four main roads and one stoplight are just two indications that life is low-key. Even the handful of shopping districts are relaxed and quiet. This is part of the attraction for visitors, who also come to hike the well marked inland footpaths, dive the offshore reefs, and laze the day away on serene, alabaster-white beaches.

LEFT:
The beach at Trunk Bay on the northwest coast is one of the ten most beautiful in the world. The underwater snorkel trail here, with signposted coral formations, is part of the 5,650 water acres that help define St. John's large national park.

OPPOSITE:
Cruz Bay, on the east coast, is one of two major centers of activity on St. John. (Coral Bay, on the west side, is the other.) Cruz Bay has a variety of shops, a ferry landing, and a seaplane port. It is small, quaint, and explored most enjoyably by foot. In the background is St. Thomas (to the right) and some small, uninhabited islands. The red and white structure in the foreground was built in 1735 to protect the town. Originally named Christianfort, it is now called The Battery and occupied by the National Park Service.

The deep-water harbor at Frederiksted was once a major export site for rum and sugar. In 1867, a tidal wave hit this area, washing away many of the town's buildings. Today, the harbor plays host to the cruise ships that come to St. Croix.

One of St. Croix's starker beauties is the calabash tree.

This mural is painted on a wall in Mongoose Junction, a charming village in the Cruz Bay area of St. John, known for its small craft shops, exceptional wares, and art studios.

A tour guide stands at one of the many windows of Whim Great House, the headquarters of one of the Dutch sugar plantations that used to cover much of St. Croix. The stone and coral wall in the foreground is three feet thick and girds the oval-shaped structure at a five-foot distance. Located near Frederiksted, the house today is a museum.

The Virgin Islands Seaplane Shuttle, which operates the largest amphibious airline in the world from its terminal in Christiansted, St. Croix, offers flights to other Virgin Islands and Puerto Rico. Using a modern, jet-propelled fleet of amphibious aircraft, it is the most direct, convenient, and enjoyable way to island-hop.

LEFT:

Trunk Bay, in the northwest, has soft sand and tranquil waters. The serenity here is complemented by moist rain forests along the shoreline that contain over a hundred varieties of thriving native plants.

This kapok (also called silk cotton) tree is at St. John's Cinnamon Bay. The sun splits the tree's thin black pods open, and the wind floats the seeds through the air. Once used locally for pillow stuffing, the seeds—at over 5,000 per pound—are still used today to fill life preservers.

Yachts and other boats, either at anchor or leisurely crossing the sea to another island, are common sights in the U.S. Virgin Islands. A number of the smaller islands—mostly uninhabited and in close proximity—offer visitors some unique exploring opportunities. Many wayfarers drop anchor to spend a night or two on the water, sleeping in rented boats before moving on to the next new world. Pictured here is Cruz Bay, St. John, where hourly ferries provide quick, inexpensive transportation to and from St. Thomas. It's not uncommon for one island's residents to commute to work on the other's shores. Some inhabitants cross the water just for a change of pace.

CURAÇAO

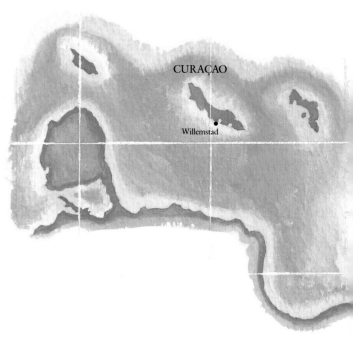

CURAÇAO

Willemstad

Curaçao is the "C" in the Dutch ABC islands that lie approximately 40 miles to the north of Venezuela. Aruba and Bonaire, the "A" and "B" members, flank, respectively, Curaçao's east and west coasts. Bonaire and Curaçao, along with Saba, St. Eustatius, and St. Maarten, located 600 miles to the northeast, form the Netherlands Antilles. Aruba used to belong to this group but is currently involved in a process that will give it independence within the Kingdom of the Netherlands. Curaçao's 171 square miles make it the largest of these six Dutch islands.

The capital city of Willemstad, on Curaçao's southern coast, is the government seat of the Netherlands Antilles. Two thirds of Curaçao's 165,000 residents live here. Named for Dutch King Willem II in

PAGE 105:

The city lights of Willemstad reflect across St. Anna Bay at night. This canal divides the city into two sections: the Punda and the Otrabanda. The two areas are connected by the Queen Emma Pontoon Bridge. First built with wood in 1888, the structure was redone in metal in 1939. The Queen Emma opens and closes approximately thirty times a day. It is the seventh largest and second busiest bridge in the world. Originally, a two-cent toll was collected from anyone who walked across the bridge with shoes on (since footwear indicated that the wearer could afford to pay). As human nature would have it, the rich took off their shoes when crossing the bridge, and the poor borrowed shoes to maintain their dignity. Today, all pedestrians use the bridge free of charge, whether they are wearing shoes or not.

OPPOSITE:

Sitting at the tip of Willemstad is the island's only highrise, the Curaçao Plaza Hotel. The foundation walls, partially seen here in the lower right corner, used to form part of a fort built in 1634. The hundreds of tankers and cruise ships that pass the Plaza every year come extremely close to the building. Covered through Lloyd's of London, it is one of two hotels in the world insured against ship collision.

Willemstad's new public library, opened in 1988, is one example of a more recent architectural design that harmonizes with the island's original Dutch colonial style.

1647, it's a charming, colorful city, with cobblestone streets, seventeenth-century buildings, and one of the busiest ports in the world. Bearing a striking resemblance to Amsterdam, it is the island's commercial, industrial, and tourist center, whose days find thousands awhirl in a shopper's paradise and whose nights are made livelier by the allure of casinos.

The island itself is mostly flat, parched, and very arid. There are some pine-covered hills in the west that rise to Mt. Cristoffel's 1,250-foot peak—the island's highest point. Some of the terrain is spotted with towering, three-armed cactus plants, while year-round trade winds lend the climate a welcome coolness and keep the indigenous divi-divi trees perpetually bent. Curaçao was formed by cooling volcanic lava, which, over time, became surrounded by large coral reefs. The caves, grottos, and beach sand along the shoreline are composed of these coral and lava deposits.

After Curaçao was discovered in 1499 by Spanish navigator Alonso de Ojeda, settlers from Spain moved in and replaced the Caiquetios Indians living there (a tribe related to the Arawaks). The Spanish remained until 1634, when the Dutch arrived and captured

OPPOSITE AND RIGHT:
Windsurfing is a sport that combines elements of surfing and sailing. The rider steers by surfing (altering the body weight on a surfboard) and maneuvering a sail that is mounted on the board. Strong breezes do the rest, and the trade winds that blow throughout the year on Curacao see that these are in no short supply. Windsurfers race across the open sea at speeds in excess of 30 miles per hour, sometimes jumping with their boards as much as eight feet into the air. Pictured on these pages are some of the twelve- to sixteen-year-old members of the Windsurfing Association—current and future entrants in Curaçao's Annual Open Windsurfing Competition, held every summer. Year round, these graceful young daredevils can be seen honing their skills after school and on weekends.

the area that is Willemstad today. Peter Stuyvesant became a governor in 1642 and stayed for three years before the Netherlands sent him to what is now New York. From the mid-1600s to the end of the eighteenth century, Britain and France tried to gain control of the island. The Treaty of Paris in 1815 finally recognized Curaçao as a Dutch possession. Simón Bolívar, who led a revolt of South American countries against Spanish rule in the early part of the nineteenth century, was granted asylum twice on the island. In 1954, the Netherlands Antilles became an autonomous part of the Kingdom of the Netherlands.

For the past few centuries, Curaçao has been an important trade center. In the mid-seventeenth century, Amsterdam controlled Europe's shipment of linen goods, and Curaçao became the natural conduit for export of these products to North and South America. Commerce increased as the African slave trade grew to its height in the early 1700s. During this time, the island served as a stopping point for slaves, who recuperated from their arduous trans-Atlantic journey and awaited transport to a final destination on another Caribbean island or South America. Because of Curaçao's arid climate, agriculture was not a major industry, and slaves were not kept here.

Today, the number-one industry is oil refining, and Curaçao is site of some of the largest refineries in the western world. Tourism ranks second. A unique product here is the bitter orange liqueur that shares the island's name. Internationally known, this after-dinner drink is made from a special kind of orange grown only on Curaçao.

Although Dutch is Curaçao's official language, a special dialect is usually spoken. Called Papiamento (from the Portuguese "papear," meaning "to jabber"), it is a blend of Dutch, Portuguese, French, Indian, and African. Over forty nationalities make up the island's population, and religious groups include Catholics, Jews, Protestants, and Muslims. Because everyone coexists peacefully, Curaçao deserves its reputation for religious and racial tolerance.

SYNAGOGUE MIKVE ISRAEL-EMANUEL

Located in downtown Willemstad, Synagogue Mikve Israel-Emanuel is the oldest synagogue in the Western Hemisphere. In 1659, twelve families of Sephardic Jews emigrated from Brazil to Holland. Because they were used to a tropical climate, the Dutch weather proved to be disagreeable, and they relocated to Curaçao. Other Jews from France, Germany, Portugal, and Brazil joined them—many seeking refuge from the horrors of the Inquisition. At first, they became farmers who cultivated sugar cane and tobacco. Within 15 years, when trading prospered, they became merchants and moved to Willemstad in a residential area known as Scharloo.

The synagogue was constructed between 1730 and 1732. It is the fourth house of worship built on its site (the first appeared in 1685) and was modeled after the oldest synagogue in Amsterdam. After its completion, Curaçao became the most important Jewish community in the Caribbean, and the 1,500 Jews that lived here comprised half of the white population on the island.

OPPOSITE:

The synagogue's interior employs a spare Dutch colonial design. The wood used throughout is mahogany, ornately carved in many places. Four antique brass chandeliers, each containing 24 candles, are modeled after similar fixtures in a Portuguese synagogue in Amsterdam. Several theories explain the sand-covered floor here. One interpretation says that the sand symbolizes the Jews' journey through the desert. Another recalls God's promise to Abraham that his descendants would be "countless as the sands of the sea." Yet another maintains that it simply serves to muffle the sound of footsteps.

The synagogue's congregation is a closely knit, reformed community from many nations. Pictured here, on the building's Spanish tile courtyard, are three members whose native lands are, from left to right, Curaçao, Venezuela, and Brooklyn, New York.

The Wedding Cake House (right) and Cerro Bonito (above) are two
landhuizen (land houses) whose original grandeur has been restored by the
island's preservation society. Open to the public and located in the Scharloo
section of Willemstad, the government owns these buildings and will
eventually occupy them.

ARCHITECTURE

In older cities throughout the world, the styles of modern buildings often contrast with those of surviving structures built long ago. Such eclecticism hardly exists on Curaçao, where Dutch colonial architecture prevails. The seventeenth-century settlers from Holland who built Willemstad modeled their new city after Amsterdam. Willemstad's forts, churches, and shops are over 200 years old. Gables and pastel purples, pinks, and yellows characterize many of the structures, which are kept scrubbed and well tended in true Dutch fashion. Streets are also impeccably clean. One of the island's early governors, said to suffer severe eyestrain from the sun's glare reflecting off the originally whitewashed buildings, is supposedly responsible for the introduction of pastel-colored paint. Whatever the case, the tradition extends to the colorful cottages in the "cunucu" (the Papiamento word for "countryside"). Windmills and thatched huts also dot the island, but the most impressive buildings are the Dutch plantation mansions, called "landhuizen" ("land houses"), which also date from the seventeenth and eighteenth centuries. Many of these are residences today, but a few are open to the public. The Netherlands has funded a great deal of the restoration work that many of these buildings have seen. Newer structures in town are carefully designed to complement the surrounding architecture. Although many stand on their own visually, the fusion of styles appears to be flawless.

Lucilia Engles' house—the only white building on the entire island—was the first to be renovated on Curaçao. This unofficially marked the beginning of the historical preservation of homes on the island.

AUTHOR'S EXCURSION: LUCILIA ENGLES

A number of serious artists and crafts people who live throughout the Caribbean don't always get the exposure they deserve, mainly because opportunities to showcase their work are often limited to island museums, galleries, and stores. Many are extremely gifted individuals whose works often reflect the unique combinations of various cultures that are found on most islands.

While shopping in Willemstad, we came across some interesting lithographs by an artist whose style was so diverse that it was hard to define. Her name is Lucilia Engles, and, when we inquired about her, we learned that she lived in town. Thinking that this would be a good opportunity to talk with one obviously talented local artist, we called to make an appointment. Lucilia graciously agreed to meet with us.

We arrived at her home in the sweltering heat of a typical Curaçao afternoon, and she immediately came to the rescue with some refreshing ice water. Her lovely home is filled with the art of Caribbean and European painters and sculptors, reflecting both her passion for art and her diverse tastes. Primarily an abstract oil painter, her images often venture into realism. She usually paints on large canvases—sometimes in muted tones, other times in vibrant colors—although she occasionally works in other media, too. One example is her 12,000-piece mosaic wall, commissioned by the Curaçao Power Company for one of its buildings. Lucilia said that she had never been interested in selling her work until Vincent Van Gogh's nephew convinced her to sell him a painting. He was so enthusiastic that he continued to send her prospective clients thereafter. To date, her exhibits have appeared in New York, Holland, Venezuela, and Santo Domingo.

In the three hours we spent together, Lucilia told us several personal stories that contribute to Curaçao's history. Her now deceased husband was the island's first permanent Dutch doctor and the only man of medicine to donate his services to the poor. In order to care for the sick and wounded during World War II, he founded the philanthropic Yellow/White Cross (the Curaçaoan equivalent of the Red Cross). She also said that he shared her passion for art and

Lucilia Engles sits in her studio near one of her more realistic paintings.

often created his own pictures while she worked on hers. One time, he secured a commission for her to paint a church mural of a white Madonna with a black Christ. Midway through the project, Lucilia became pregnant, eventually giving birth to twins. The church laity considered this a miracle, since Lucilia and her husband had been trying, without success, to conceive for twelve years. The church became known as "The Chapel of the Twins." Today, the Engles' daughter—one of the "miracle" twins—is curator of the Curaçao Museum, which Lucilia and her husband established.

FLOATING MARKET

Two centuries ago, fishermen and farmers from South America began sailing across the short stretch of Caribbean Sea to Curaçao, where they sold their goods to Dutch settlers. Today, this practice still takes place in the heart of Willemstad. Boats laden with fruits and vegetables stay as long as a week so that farmers can merchandise their produce. Fishing vessels arrive with greater frequency, selling their cargo of snapper, conch, and yellowtail, then venturing back out to the open sea to replenish their stock.

OPPOSITE:
Floating-market boats tie up along a small canal in Willemstad. The red-tile roof of the building in the background is a typical Dutch colonial feature.

LEFT:
Mangoes, papayas, and other exotic fruits and vegetables of the floating market are set up along Willemstad's wharf. Shoppers and vendors generally barter over prices.

BEACHES

Beaches on Curaçao are small, intimate, and accessible. There are over three dozen public and private spots of hardpacked coral and lava sand that nestle in coves, inlets, and lagoons around the island. The better beaches for swimming, snorkeling, and boating are along the southeast, where the shore is protected from the trade winds. Often crowded on weekends, they are usually peaceful and private during the rest of the week.

LEFT:

Curaçao is ringed with small coves, and Knip Bay is one of the largest. Located in the northwest near the town of Westpunt, Knip Bay is backed by sheer cliffs and protected from trade winds. This, combined with tranquil waters and a well stocked snack bar, make it one of the most popular public beaches on the island.

OPPOSITE:

Throughout the Caribbean, residents often vacation on their own islands. The Curaçaoan children pictured were on a seaside holiday with their families and had rented rooms in a nearby hotel.

ST. MARTIN ST. MAARTEN

Grand Case

ST. MARTIN

Marigot

Philipsburg

ST. MAARTEN

St. Martin/St. Maarten is the smallest territory in the world to be shared by two sovereign states. Its 37 square miles are bisected by a jagged horizontal boundary: the 21 square miles to the north comprise St. Martin, a French West Indies subprefect of France, while the 16 square miles to the south is St. Maarten, part of the Netherlands Antilles. People are permitted free travel between the two sections and do not encounter customs officials, border guards, or other barriers. Only a single monument, erected in 1948 and bearing a welcome sign in French and English, lets a visitor know that the dividing line has been crossed.

Columbus claimed the island for Spain when he discovered it in 1493. Dutch and French settlers arrived in the early 1630s and fought with Spain, who won but eventually abandoned the island. A treaty signed on November 11, 1648, divided the island between France and the Netherlands, although its present division was established in 1816.

St. Martin/St. Maarten is a hilly limestone island with a coastline of white beaches outlining large and small bays. In the southwest, a narrow strip of land several miles long extends from the Dutch mainland and arcs around to reconnect at the French sector; the large body of water in the middle is Simpson Bay Lagoon, where various

Tourist accommodations on St. Martin/St. Maarten, as well as on most other islands in the Caribbean, run the gamut from big luxury resorts to small efficiency units. This imposing villa, located in St. Maarten's Little Bay area, is rented on a time-share basis.

OPPOSITE:
This St. Maarten beach, at Little Bay on the southern coast, is one of approximately three dozen cozy stretches that ring the island. To the west, Cupecoy Bay Beach is lined with caves and sandstone cliffs, while Oriental Bay Beach up the eastern coast in the French section is the island's best known spot for nude sunbathing.

popular water sports are enjoyed. The waters around the entire island are so clear that depth visibility is often as much as 100 feet.

Thirty thousand people live on the island, with the largest concentrations found in each section's capital city: Philipsburg on the Dutch side (with a government seat in Willemstad on Curaçao) and Marigot on the French (under the jurisdiction of Basse-Terre on Guadeloupe). St. Martin, with its bistros, small hotels, relaxed way of life, and superb French cuisine, retains the special flavor of its homeland, while Dutch St. Maarten mixes the pastel-colored buildings and flower-bedecked streets of the Netherlands with a fast pace and jet-set life style that are distinctly American. English, although not the official language in either area, is predominant in both.

St. Martin/St. Maarten is a playground, and it is for this reason that tourism reigns supreme. A good three quarters of the population work in the tourist industry in jobs ranging from hotel, restaurant, and nightclub operations, to water sports equipment and boat rentals. People come here to relax, have fun, and mingle in an international setting that is decidedly chic.

ST. MARTIN/ST. MAARTEN'S DAY

St. Martin/St. Maarten's Day is observed every November 11th in honor of that date in 1648, when the Dutch and French signed a treaty recognizing the boundary between their two sectors. Before signing, the Dutch and French islanders had repeatedly tried to convince their homeland governments of the treaty's value. When a last attempt failed, they signed anyway.

A Dutch soldier and a French policeman grab a few moments of conversation before the official proceedings get underway. The simple ceremony involves the laying of a wreath at the Border Monument by Dutch and French officials—an act that formally renews their pledge for continued amicable relations.

Popular legend has it that a gin-swigging Dutch representative and a wine-swilling French delegate set out on foot in opposite directions from Oyster Bay on the east coast. Walking the circumference of the island—with the Frenchman covering slightly more territory—they met at Cupecoy Bay on the west coast, thus establishing the two ends of the dividing line.

Although the British occupied the island several times since, the Dutch and French still recognize 1648 as the official year that launched over three centuries of peaceful coexistence. Each year's observance, also called Concordia Day, takes place at Mt. Concordia, where the treaty was signed. After the ceremony, some rather low-key celebrations take place, including parties, dances, concerts, road races, and regattas.

One of Jean-Pierre's falcons sits on a perch in the shade. Some of the larger birds are kept in cages when they're not performing.

We learned about falconer Jean-Pierre Bodes and his birds-of-prey show from a flyer in our hotel. Having read that there are only seven such shows in the world, with six in Europe and the seventh on St. Maarten, we were intrigued. We called Jean-Pierre to make an appointment.

He agreed to give us a private viewing, since only one show had been scheduled for that day. (Usually, shows are held twice daily, since the birds themselves naturally hunt that often.) We arrived on his grounds in St. Maarten in the late afternoon. Walking across the lawn, I suddenly saw a swooping shape out of the corner of my eye. I instinctively ducked, then realized that I was not in danger. I stood up, held out my arm, and three lightweight Caribbean Kestrel Falcons landed so lightly that it was hard to believe that they had talons.

Jean-Pierre welcomed us graciously when we walked through the gate and invited us to sit down and talk for a few minutes over a glass of beer. He told us that falconing is only pursued by a handful of people today. Birds are scarce, usually supplied by zoos, and they require a great deal of time and care to train, he said. Extra time and care must be given to the birds to prevent the onset of illness. His own interest was sparked in Europe 25 years ago by a friend, and he has been training birds of prey ever since.

The show began. Each species of bird was brought out separately—starting with the smallest and building to the largest—so that Jean-Pierre could discuss its unique characteristics. The Caribbean Kestrel Falcon, with an average weight of 3.5 ounces, is the smallest bird of prey in the world. The two-pound Peregrine Falcon is the fastest, attaining speeds of 200 miles per hour when diving. We saw this spectacular bird make one such dive when Jean-Pierre swung a lure of chicken meat attached to the end of a rawhide strip. Peregrines have a life span of 25 years and are the only birds of prey that cannot hunt on the ground due to their high speeds. Kites, falcons, eagles, and other hawks were introduced. Some headed into the sky to catch flying lures of chicken meat. We

Jean-Pierre Bodes, the falconer, holds an American Fisher Eagle just before he sets it free to perform.

were given gloves and food so that others could land on our hands and be fed. Then came the vultures. With wing spans of up to nine feet, these are the largest birds of prey. They are peculiar-looking and have a life expectancy of 80 years. We thought there was something comedic about them as they loped along on the ground following Jean-Pierre. The finale was an aerial ballet of sorts, as each species—about 20 in all—took a "curtain call," flying one after another to secure a final chicken snack from Jean-Pierre.

Two features were especially intriguing. First was the fact that the birds were completely free. Any one of them could have vanished into the wilds, yet time and again, with familial-like devotion, each one chose to remain with Jean-Pierre, who explained that the birds are very territorial about their land. Second was the opportunity to hold and feed the same wild creatures that we had previously only seen in zoos, on TV, and in magazines and books.

RESTAURANTS

One of the main reasons people come to St. Martin/St. Maarten is the food. Dining is so popular that it's a favorite topic of conversation among visitors—not surprising, considering that there are over 200 restaurants that offer a fantastic selection of high-quality dishes in all price ranges.

Most restaurants are concentrated in Philipsburg and Marigot, but excellent meals can be found throughout the island as well. The small fishing village of Grand Case, northeast of Marigot, has a mile-long main street that has been dubbed "The Restaurant Capital of the Caribbean." Most of the two dozen or so international eating establishments in Grand Case offer a variety of superb foods on lovely seaside terraces.

From buttery escargots to spicy fish stews, both classic and creole French cuisine is a favorite throughout the entire island. Dutch cooking is harder to come by but not impossible to find. Whether washed down with vintage French wine or stout Dutch beer, some of the most sophisticated meals in the Caribbean are here, prepared by chefs from such places as Italy, the Far East, and Indonesia. Every restaurant's ambience gives diners the feeling that they are being personally welcomed into someone's home.

The West Indian Tavern, located on Front Street in Philipsburg, is one of the few remaining examples of nineteenth-century Dutch architecture on St. Maarten. The fretwork and gingerbreading are motifs of the Victorian era.

OPPOSITE:

The restaurant Jean Dupont in Marigot is named for its owner. A table setting typifies a theme that is popular island-wide: simple elegance with a promise of a pleasant, leisurely dining experience to come. Dupont and his wife Evelyn also run La Santal just west of Marigot, a restaurant reputed to have some of the best French cuisine on St. Martin.

Just off Front Street is a new minimall where a wide selection of clothes, giftwares, and artwork can be found. The multicolored, narrow store fronts, reminiscent of Holland, are typical of Philipsburg and can be found both along Front and Back Streets and the steegjes (little lanes) that connect them.

SHOPPING

Dutch Philipsburg and, to a lesser extent, French Marigot are two of the busiest and best shopping hubs in the Caribbean. The fact that the entire island is duty-free, coupled with an absence of local taxes, helps explain why there are so many top-quality bargains here. Merchants set their own prices, and while some items retail at costs comparable to those elsewhere in the world, many others can be found at discounts of up to 50 percent.

Philipsburg is by far the shopping mecca. The town is situated in south St. Maarten on an isthmus between Great Salt Pond and Great Bay. Front Street, the main shopping thoroughfare, runs parallel to Back Street, the other commercial byway. The former is usually clogged with traffic, and shopping is best done on foot. The stores—some in modern buildings, others in colorful Dutch houses—sell everything from inexpensive trinkets to costly luxury items. Merchandise ranges from European china and crystal and exotic Far East embroideries to top Italian fashions, Japanese gadgetry, and fine Swiss watches.

Although Marigot can also bulge with shoppers—especially when cruise ships are in—this town is smaller and more relaxed. Located on St. Martin's west coast, Marigot is characterized by boutiques, bistros, and grillwork balconies. Many of the good buys here—including perfume, cosmetics, and fashions—are top-notch French imports.

Though usually crowded, Philipsburg's streets, courtyards, alleys, and patios are colorful, cheerful, and clean. Store owners accentuate these qualities by displaying merchandise in careful and sometimes unusual ways.

131

GAMBLING

Gambling on St. Maarten is not pursued with the maniacal fervor typically found in most of the world's wagering capitals. The accent here is on leisure.

While gambling is popular among both the Dutch and the French, it takes place only on the Dutch side of the island. Players must be eighteen or older if they want to try their luck at blackjack, roulette, the slot machines, and other games of chance. Most of St. Maarten's nine casinos have hours from 8 PM to 3 AM, but, whenever cruise ships are in the harbor, doors will open as early as one o'clock in the afternoon. Some casinos are small and intimate, while others, with their spacious interiors, live music, and sports-betting boards, have all the glamor and glitz of Las Vegas.

A wide assortment of boating vessels attests to the variety of seagoing excursions that are available on St. Martin/ St. Maarten. Catamaran tours, sailing lessons, and evening cruises provide only half the picture, for there are also several types of watercraft, such as cutters, ketches, yachts, and motorboats, that can be rented for day trips to neighboring islands. St. Kitts and Nevis, at 44 miles away, are perhaps too far for a quick jaunt, but the distances to St. Eustatius (35 miles), Saba (27 miles), St. Barts (14 miles), and Anguilla (4.6 miles) put the natural environments of these islands within easy reach.

MARTINIQUE

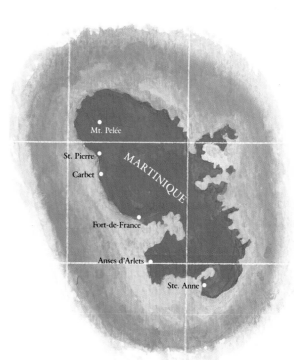

Mt. Pelée

St. Pierre

Carbet

MARTINIQUE

Fort-de-France

Anses d'Arlets

Ste. Anne

MARTINIQUE

Martinique was originally named "Madinina" by the Carib Indians who lived there. The word means "Isle of Flowers," and it accurately describes this beautiful island that today remains covered with such vibrant floral forms as the scarlet trumpets of the hibiscus blossoms and the star-shaped yellows and pinks of frangipani blooms. These and many other exquisite tropical flowers not only blanket the island but also make a small contribution to its economy.

Martinique is scenic for other reasons, too. Primarily mountainous, especially in the north, the island was formed by volcanoes. The largest, Mt. Pelée, rises from the northwest shore to a height of 4,656 feet. The more centrally located Carbet Peaks, covered by a network of rivers and streams, are only slightly smaller. Northern rain forests and inland cane fields cover most of the island's 427 square miles in a wash of lush green, while a flatter, more arid south is characterized by salt marshes, cactus, and fine white sand. A craggy, cove-pocked Atlantic coastline contrasts with a smoother western shore that is broken only by the wide, miles-long harbor of Fort-de-France Bay.

Columbus sighted the island in 1502 but didn't stay because of hostile Carib Indians, who maintained control until 1635. In that year, Pierre Belain d'Esnambuc, a Norman nobleman, landed with a group of settlers and built Fort Saint-Pierre, a stronghold that managed to withstand fierce attacks from the Caribs. France and Britain fought frequently for possession of Martinique over the next

PAGE 137:
A bristly pineapple field sits along a road traveling northeast from St. Pierre to the town of Morne Rouge. Pineapple exports have become a major industry on Martinique, and canning the fruit has helped it to become the third largest agricultural endeavor, after sugar cane and bananas. Most pineapple crops are grown in the northern part of the island.

OPPOSITE:
Farms, plantations, and ranches blanket Martinique's northern countryside. This section of the island is just outside St. Pierre.

A mountain road that connects St. Pierre with the north-central village of Morne Rouge passes through a number of villages. Certain trees and flowers seem to lend each town its own color scheme and look. A row of fan tail palms and poinsettia plants put the stamp of individuality on the final section of the road that leads into Morne Rouge.

200 years, with the British only occupying it for three relatively brief periods. Finally, in 1815, the Treaty of Paris recognized the island as a French possession. In 1946, Martinique became an overseas département (province) of France. The people, known as Martiniquais, became full French citizens in 1974, when the island was officially designated as a French région (territory).

The modern culture is extremely French-influenced—a fact reflected in the cuisine, the perfumes and fashions sold in stores, and the language, which includes both standard French and Creole patois. Tourism is a major industry, and the island's French flavor makes Martinique especially popular among European visitors. Most of the 350,000 residents are Roman Catholic and enjoy a high standard of living that includes free schooling, good roads, and government-sponsored medical care. Approximately one third of them live in the west-coast capital city of Fort-de-France, the island's commercial and cultural center that is also a major cruise-ship port.

When Mt. Pelée erupted on May 8, 1902, it had not given the residents of St. Pierre any warning signs. Instead, it exploded with smoke, ash, rock, and lava that blanketed the town in temperatures reaching 3,000 degrees Centigrade. In approximately three minutes, the entire population—a total of 30,000 people—was dead, and only ruins and ashes remained. The sole survivor was a prisoner named Louis Cyparis, whose underground, thick-walled jail cell saved his life.

The Musée Volcanologique is a museum in St. Pierre, founded by American Frank A. Perret, that documents the disaster. Photographs and stories detail the former grandeur of the city as well as the aftermath. Relics dug from the debris are on display and include melted silverware, petrified spaghetti, and twisted clocks whose faces were stopped at 8:00 AM when Pelée erupted.

Mt. Pelée's peak, at 4,656 feet, is the highest point on Martinique. Hikers wanting to climb the mountain usually find that it's a four- or five-hour trip from St. Pierre. Although the volcano is quiet today, it is not extinct. As a precaution against future catastrophe, scientists keep the volcano closely monitored.

St. Pierre was once nicknamed "Little Paris of the West Indies" when it served as Martinique's capital city. That all changed when Mt. Pelée, whose peak here hides behind a cloud, erupted and left everything in ruins. Today, St. Pierre is a picturesque village with a population that is one fourth what it used to be.

A sobering testament to Mt. Pelée's eruption is the ruins of a fashionable theater modeled after the Grand Théâtre in Bordeaux, France. Pictured is what remains of the theater's entrance.

Sailing is a favorite activity in Martinique, and the marina at Poite du Bout is the primary sailboat headquarters. Other vessels available for rental include motorboats and yachts, and hour-long underwater excursions take sightseers beneath sea level. Ferries from Fort-de-France dock here as well, putting travelers within walking distance of Martinique's hotel and restaurant center.

OPPOSITE:
Anses d'Arlets is a fishing village on Martinique's southwest coast. The crayon-colored boats drawn up onto the sand form a typical scene on the island's Caribbean coast.

Pictured is one of the hibiscus flowers in Balata Gardens. This red variety is seen primarily in the Caribbean region.

OPPOSITE:
Balata Gardens boasts a magnificent bed of anthuriums. This tropical flower is also known as a flamingo plant and a painter's palette.

Balata Gardens, located at the base of a rain forest, is a 20-minute drive north of Fort-de-France. Over a thousand varieties of plant life are here—some indigenous to Martinique, others imported from such areas as India, China, Japan, New Zealand, and South America. The planning that has gone into Balata Gardens makes it one of the most beautifully tended grounds in the Caribbean. Created by Jean-Philippe Thoze, the landscaping juxtaposes flowers and trees of contrasting colors, shapes, and textures. Thoze began collecting the various floral species in the 1960s and spent over 20 years bringing the gardens to their present splendor. The property used to belong to his grandmother and includes her beautifully restored country home on its site. Named for the tropical trees here that produce a latex-like sap, Balata Gardens covers several acres, contains lovely shaded paths and several benches, and offers pleasing views of the Carbet Peaks to the north and Fort-de-France to the south.

Le Parc de Floralies is a small botanical garden on the Pagerie plantation grounds. In it stands a statue of the Empress Josephine.

OPPOSITE:
Marie-Josèphe Rose Tascher de la Pagerie, better known to most as Napoleon's Empress Josephine, was born in 1763 near Martinique's town of Trois-Ilets. The sugar plantation, where she lived until the age of 16, was destroyed by a hurricane in 1860, but the stone building that served as the family kitchen, pictured here, still stands. It is known today as the Pagerie Museum and displays portraits of Napoleon and Josephine, love letters and other personal papers, medals, bills, and Josephine's original furniture.

In Fort-de-France, across the street from the Flamingo Bay *ferry landing, is the town's 12½-acre public park. Called La Savane, it is a beautiful blend of open space and tree-covered footpaths, accented by well trimmed gardens and plenty of benches. Surrounding the park are such diversions as an open craft market, snack trucks, cafés, and shops. On the bay side is a bumper-car pavilion, while across the park can be found a carousel and a climbing area for children. Every morning by 9:00 AM, a group of workers have finished clearing the grounds of debris and fallen leaves and branches.*

OPPOSITE:

Les Salines Beach is located just outside Ste. Anne. Bordered by coconut palms, this is the island's most beautiful beach. On many French Caribbean beaches, topless bathing is the norm, and Les Salines is no exception. However, it does have one unique feature: the food vendors, who begin setting up their stands at about 10:00 AM each day, bring tables and chairs so that their customers can sit and snack in extra comfort. Les Salines, French for "salt marshes," describes a topographical characteristic of Martinique's southern coast.

A small traveling carnival claimed a section of the Fort-de-France waterfront for a six-to-eight-week engagement. The carnival tours other Caribbean islands for stints of equal duration. Pointe du Bout and its cove, Anse du Bout, are among the distant hills pictured in the background.

OPPOSITE:
Diamond Rock sits two and a half miles off the shore of Le Diamant, a town on Martinique's southern coast. In 1804, over a hundred British sailors manned the rock and, for eighteen months, fought the French, who were stationed on land. The British Navy officially registered the rock as a ship of war, naming it the "HMS Diamond Rock." Nearly 600 feet high, it is covered with cactus and brush and today serves as a refuge for thousands of birds.

AUTHOR'S EXCURSION: CARNIVAL

In the Christian calendar, Lent is the 40-day period of fasting and penitence that begins on Ash Wednesday and ends with Easter. Traditionally, Carnival is the joyful holiday that takes place during Shrovetide, the three days preceding Ash Wednesday. Virtually all the islands in the Caribbean celebrate Carnival in one form or another. Some put it off until the spring, while others wait as late as August. Martinique follows the Christian tradition, with one notable exception: instead of ending the festivities on the day before Ash Wednesday, the islanders here extend their merrymaking an extra 24 hours, waiting until Thursday to begin their solemn observance of Lent.

Carnival is the most festive time of year on Martinique. Every town on the island has its own celebration, with the greatest activity concentrated in Fort-de-France. Called "Vaval" by Martiniquais, Carnival actually begins in January, right after Epiphany, which commemorates the day centuries ago when the divine nature of Christ was revealed to the three magi. Each village begins to construct floats and make costumes in preparation for the final four days. Parties and special events are held on the six weekends that span the time between Epiphany and Lent. Creole song contests are held, and each town's Carnival Queen is elected. Then, on the Sunday before Ash Wednesday, the big, half-week-long finale begins.

Our hotel overlooked La Savane in Fort-de-France, where Carnival would be held. On Sunday afternoon, we came outdoors early so that I could get a feel for the area and perhaps take some pre-parade photographs, but the park was relatively empty. Most

of the activity was centered in an area just north of La Savane, and we photographed our way into the crowd. Suddenly, without warning, Carnival began. Author Truman Capote wrote about Martinique's Carnival, saying that its commencement was "as spontaneous as an explosion in a fireworks factory," and that's exactly what it was like. The sounds of drums and horns echoed off the city walls. Our senses seemed to heighten, and we became slightly intoxicated by the intensity of all the activity.

The parade moved through town, and we followed. Decorated floats edged their way through the crowd of wall-to-wall people. We caught a glimpse of the Carnival Queen perched on top of one float, but she soon became lost in the singing, dancing, clamoring masses. Spectators became participants. Vendors sold food from their stands along the fringes. Side streets swarmed with newcomers who effortlessly formed

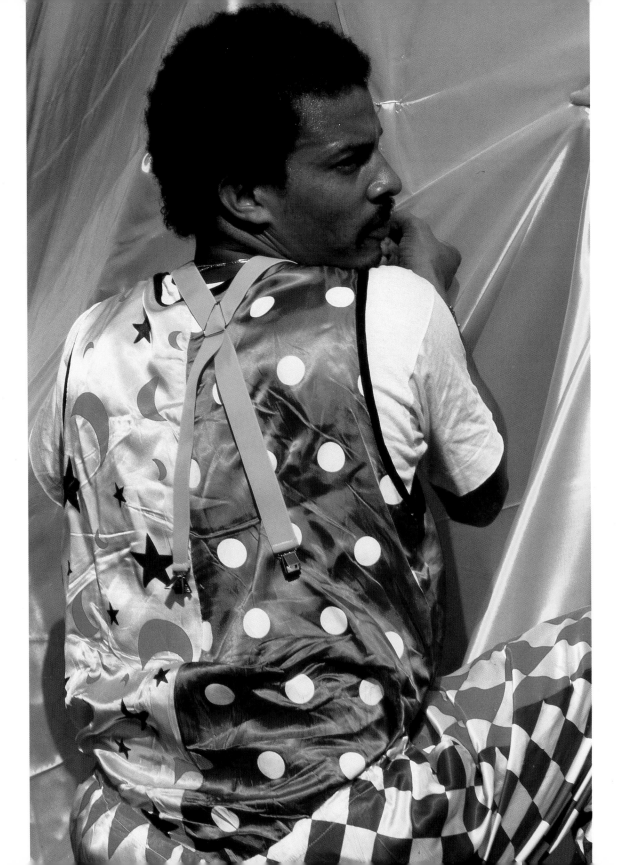

into small processions that fed into the larger sea of anonymous movement and swirling color. The parade had begun at 3:30 and continued for four hours. By evening, we were exhausted, but the revelers had only just begun. Public merrymaking became indoor carousing, as groups of people dressed in costumes made their way to private parties and masquerade balls that would last through the night.

Monday was Round Two. We decided to have lunch in a pizza parlor in Fort-de-France. Our waitress told us that on this particular day a bigger, more grandiose celebration would take place in the town of Le François on Martinique's east coast. Since the town was only 10 miles away and we had the time to get there, we thanked her for her hot tip and went to get the car.

Arriving in Le François, we found the main section of town closed to traffic, with cars lining the sides of roads for miles in all directions. We claimed a parking space about a mile and a half from where we wanted to be and walked the distance into town. Tens of thousands of people filled the streets and carried on as they paraded through town. This day of Carnival is unofficially nicknamed "Burlesque Monday." Many of the celebrants were dressed in wedding gowns and camped it up as they marched through the streets. Most of these flamboyant "brides-to-be" were men, and their ribald antics were special crowd-pleasers.

The next day, Shrove Tuesday, we rejoined the throngs in Fort-de-France. This is the traditional Mardi Gras ("Fat Tuesday") that ends most other Carnivals. Once again, the streets filled with dancers, musicians, minstrels, and other merrymakers. The parade was less organized than Sunday's, spilling through the town and following no particular route. The day is nicknamed "Red-Devil Day," and many of the participants wore devil costumes—some simply in their brightest red clothing, others in masks and elaborate get-ups. Children and adults alike were devils for the day, cavorting and rejoicing with abandon. The energy seemed more frenetic than it had on the previous two days, and we marveled at the inexhaustible reserves everyone seemed to possess. When evening drew near, the clamoring came to a halt, and the festivities moved inside for another round of all-night parties.

Ash Wednesday's theme is "Festival of the She-Devils," which requires everyone to wear only black and white. Even faces, hands, and legs are painted in these colors. The pace of this day was the most frantic yet. "Rejoice today and repent tomorrow" was everyone's motto, and staminas were pushed to the limit, as though the crowd was collectively building toward some ritualistic climax. That moment came shortly after the final parade passed through town. This march was a funeral procession for King Vaval and his crony Bois-Bois, two life-size, papier-mâché figures, who were carried to a funeral pyre in La Savane. As the fire was lit and the flames burned, "she-devils" of both sexes danced at fever pitch. Finally, long past sunset, an entourage of pall bearers led the coffin to its gravesite, burying King Vaval and ending Carnival for another year.

The next day, the vendors had left and the streets and park grounds were spotless. All traces of Carnival were gone. Everyone had come to party, and they did it very well. The revels had celebrated the unbridled, earthy side of human nature, and it was done in a spirit of camaraderie that lingered.

157